S I A

ALL THE RUSSIAS

FITZROY

THE

SIAS

MACLEAN

SMITHMARK

For
Katharine

Text and photographs:
FITZROY MACLEAN

Originated and developed by
BATO TOMAŠEVIĆ

Design:
GANE ALEKSIĆ

Appendix research:
MARIJA & BRANISLAV MARKOVIĆ

Editor:
MADGE PHILLIPS

Endpaper design:
ZORAN MUJBEGOVIĆ

Printed and bound in Slovenia by
DELO, Ljubljana

CONTENTS

FOREWORD

More than ever before is the attention of the world focussed on what was formerly known as the Soviet Union, at present undergoing what Mikhail Gorbachov described as 'a period of revolutionary change', which now seems likely to end in its virtual disintegration. What, long term, does the future hold for what is still nominally the biggest country in the world? How far will its present rulers seek to retain any degree of control over it? What measure of interdependence will continue to exist between its constituent republics, now in the grip of overwhelmingly strong nationalist and separatist movements? What, in short, are the former Soviet Union's prospects of holding together at all?

First, it is necessary to grasp the immense extent of the Soviet Union and the enormous diversity of the peoples and races who inhabit it. To recall, too, the manner in which, at one time or another, they became incorporated in it. And to realise that the former Russian Empire was the result of more than three centuries of sustained expansion, northwards, southwards, eastwards and westwards. While other European powers founded colonies overseas, the Russians, for their part, were reaching out across two continents, vastly extending their territories at the expense of their immediate neighbours. 'All the Russias,' wrote Gogol, 'the land that has spread smoothly, gliding over half the earth.' Today, a good deal less smoothly, the process is being reversed.

F. M.

THE ORIGINS

The origins of Russia or Rus, the ethnic Russian heartland, were relatively modest. The tribes which early in the Middle Ages eventually settled in what are now the fertile plains of European Russia were Slavs, attracted there from further east by the network of natural waterways which linked the Baltic and the Black Sea, and by the opportunities these offered for trade. But for a long time after their arrival the whole region was to remain in a state of turmoil, and these early Slav settlers and traders had to contend with innumerable difficulties, not least the fresh waves of invaders who continued to sweep down on Russia from the Asian landmass.

It was for this reason that in the ninth century of our era the inhabitants of one of their earliest settlements, Novgorod or New Town in northern Russia, feeling, as Slavs have periodically felt throughout their history, the need for firmer and better government and stronger defences, turned for help and advice to their northern neighbours, the Varangians or Vikings. 'Our land,' they declared, 'is great and rich. But there is no order in it. Come and rule over us.' The Varangians did not wait to be asked twice. Soon the Viking Prince Rurik had made himself ruler of Novgorod and so founded Russia's first ruling dynasty, the Rurikids, who, for their part, gradually became ever more closely assimilated to the Russians they ruled over.

Like most Vikings, Rurik and his kin were conquerors. Moving southwards from Novgorod, they quickly extended their dominions as far as Kiev on the Dnieper, Mother of Russian Cities and now principal city of the Ukraine, which in time became the capital of a loose confederation of autonomous principalities known collectively as Rus. Russia, it is said, was born between two seas. For her rulers it was essential to keep open their trade routes between the Baltic in the north and the Black Sea in the south. Each spring the ruling prince, accompanied by a well-armed retinue or *druzhina*, would sail southwards with a flotilla of cargo-vessels, down the broad stream of the River Dnieper and on across the Black Sea to Byzantium, then capital of the Eastern Empire. By 967, the whole length of the mighty River Volga had likewise been brought under Russian control.

With time, the contacts between pagan Kiev and Christian Byzantium grew ever closer. In 988 Rurik's grandson, Vladimir, married Anna, sister of the co-Emperors of Byzantium, and was himself soon converted to Christianity. In due course he was canonised and today his statue, holding aloft a great bronze cross, looks thoughtfully out across the Dnieper, in whose waters he caused his loyal subjects to be baptised in droves. A ruthless and dynamic ruler popularly known as *fornicator immensus,* Saint Vladimir first gave Kievan Rus the character of a state. Apart from its spiritual significance, his conversion to Christianity was of great political importance. Closely linked with Byzantium and freely exposed to its civilising influence, Kievan Rus became in time an integral part of Christian Europe. The reigns of Vladimir and his son, Yaroslav the Wise, marked the peak of the cultural, economic and political achievement of Kievan Rus. Seeking to make of Kiev a fitting capital for the confederation over which he ruled, Yaroslav built on the heights overlooking the Dnieper the great cathedral church of Saint Sophia and the adjoining Monastery of the Caves.

Yaroslav the Wise was the last grand prince to rule effectively over the whole of Kievan Rus. On his death in 1054, a fierce struggle broke out for the succession, and the loose confederation of principalities over which he had presided began to fall apart. Fresh waves of nomad invaders now flooded into Russia. But, instead of combining against them, the individual Russian princes bickered ineffectually among themselves, while more and more of their unhappy subjects sought safety in the forests of the north. Still further north, meanwhile, on the Baltic, fresh enemies of Russia were emerging: Teutonic Knights, Lithuanians and Swedes.

With Kiev's decline, power passed elsewhere. By the beginning of the thirteenth century two powerful principalities had come into being in Russia. In the north, Rurik's old capital of Novgorod, by now bigger than any other Russian city and possessing dominions greater than all the rest of Russia put together, was democratically governed by a *veche* or assembly of citizens who themselves elected both prince and archbishop. Some hundreds of miles away to the south-east lay Rostov-Suzdal, likewise a land of forests, ruled over until his death in 1157 by Prince Yuri Dolgoruki or Long-in-the-Arm, who, during the thirty-odd years of his reign, founded within its borders the new townships of Vladimir, Yaroslavl, Pereslavl-Zalesski and finally Moscow, then no more than a lonely wooden stockade on a little hill above the river of the same name.

On Yuri's death he was succeeded by his son, Andrei of Bogolyubovo. Andrei was a warrior, a man of considerable culture and a future saint. For his capital he chose the new town of Vladimir and, summoning 'master-craftsmen from all countries', endowed it with a number of magnificent churches, built from the local limestone, though perhaps the most beautiful of them all was the simple little Church of the Intercession, which he built nearby in his own village of Bogolyubovo. After which, having raised a powerful army, he sacked Novgorod and Kiev and, returning in triumph to Vladimir, boldly assumed the title of grand prince.

But Prince Andrei was not to enjoy the fruits of his victories or his fine new capital for long. In 1175 he was murdered by some dissident boyars, acting in collusion with his beautiful wife Ulita, whose father he had slain and who, it seems, had always hated him. As grand prince he was succeeded by his brother Vsevolod, known,

3. *View of the Kremlin from the Moskva River, with the Borovitski Tower (nearest), the nineteenth-century Kremlin Palace, and older churches (fifteenth–sixteenth century) in the background, dominated by the lofty bell-tower of Ivan the Great.*

4. *Entrance to Red Square from the Marx Prospekt, with the Kremlin walls on the right, and part of the Moscow Historical Museum on the left. Red Square, for centuries the heart of Russia, is always crowded with tourists visiting the historic buildings of the Kremlin, the Cathedral of St Basil, and GUM department store.*

5. *Monument to Minin and Pozharski on Red Square, raised in 1818 to honour the two leaders of the Russian struggle against Polish invasion in the early seventeenth century. Kuzma Minin, an illiterate merchant from Novgorod, together with Prince Dmitri Pozharski, an able general, led the popular uprising against the Poles in 1611 that ended in their expulsion.*

6. *Towers of the Moscow Kremlin (citadel). In the late thirteenth century it was encircled by earthen walls and a palisade, replaced in the fourteenth by walls and towers of white marble, and reinforced by brick walls in the fifteenth century. The ornamental spires were a seventeenth-century addition. Most famous of the gate towers is the Spasski (Redeemer).*

7–10. *War veterans decked out in medals for an anniversary celebration. Though nearly half a century has passed since the Second World War, it remains firmly imprinted in the hearts and minds of the people. Of the 55 millions who died in that war, over 20 millions were Soviet citizens. The ageing war veterans are still accorded full honour and recognition for their military services.*

11–14. GUM (an acronym for State Universal Store) on Red Square. Its basic plan of a rectangular area with galleries dates back to the sixteenth–seventeenth century. In the eighteenth–nineteenth century it grew into a rectangular building with several floors. The interior is now divided into a number of 'streets' with many small shops, all covered by a single glass roof. GUM is visited by one and a half million customers daily.

15. The Kremlin cathedrals seen from the Moskva River. These magnificent churches were raised in the fifteenth and sixteenth centuries, when Muscovy was growing into a powerful centralised state with Moscow as its capital and seat of its rulers. Today the Kremlin is a unique museum of eight centuries of Russian history and art. (pp. 20–21)

16. *Part of the Cathedral Square in the Kremlin: right, the fifteenth-century Rizopolozheniye, church of the Russian metropolitans.*

17. *Cathedral of the Annunciation, raised in the Kremlin in the 1480s by architects and masons from Pskov on the site of an earlier church. The ikons by Andrei Rublov on the ikonostasis of the old cathedral were preserved in the new one.*

18. Changing the guard of honour in front of Lenin's Mausoleum on Red Square, close to the Kremlin walls. The original tomb, built of wood in 1924, was replaced six years later by a more impressive stone structure faced with marble, granite, porphyry and labradorite.

20. Young Moscow parents, many living in cramped or shared flats, spend much of their time taking the children for walks and outings. Russians in general dote on children, though the birth-rate in cities is low. Parents take their role very seriously.

19. A call to action from beyond the tomb. Until recently, Soviet towns and villages were smothered in posters, slogans, wall newspapers, proclamations and the like, all intended to galvanize the masses for the latest tasks set by their government.

25

21. *Arkhagelskoye Palace near Moscow, built for Prince Golitsyn in the early eighteenth century. From 1810 to 1917 it belonged to the Yusupov family, and in 1918 become a museum. The estate was famous for its park, a copy of Versailles.*

22. *The old neo-classical building of Moscow's M. V. Lomonosov University (MGU), the largest in Rusia and one of the world's leading centres of scientific research. Founded in 1755 on the initiative of the eminent scientist Lomonosov, it has grown into a gigantic institution with some 300,000 students. The new university building on the Lenin Heights has 55,000 rooms.*

23. *Moscow old and new. In 1987 the city celebrated the 800th anniversary of its foundation. (pp. 28–29)*

24. *Cupolas of the Cathedral of the Redeemer (Spasski Sobor), second of the great churches to be built within the Kremlin, in 1330, four years after the old Uspenski Sobor. (pp. 30–31)*

25. *A typical product of 1950s 'Stalinist' architecture. Grandiose buildings in this style include the Ukraine Hotel and Lomonosov University on Lenin Heights.*

26. *Red Square by night: Lenin's Mausoleum backed by the mighty walls of the Kremlin – the mecca of all tourists visiting Moscow. The huge scale of the square and citadel suggests the vast expanse of the Russian Empire and Soviet state.*

27. The Emperor Bell, the largest in the world, nearly 20 feet high and weighing 200 tons, was cast in 1733–35. As a result of a fire two years later, an 11-ton piece broke off, and the bell lay abandoned until placed on its present site in the Kremlin in 1836. It has never been rung.

28. *The Emperor Cannon,
standing not far from the bell, is
another mammoth curiosity.
Cast in 1586, it is 17.5 feet long
and weighs 40 tons. Intended
for defence of the Kremlin, like
the bell it has never been used.*

29. Cathedral of the Annunciation, Moscow. Though one of the largest of the Kremlin churches, it leaves an impression of lightness, thanks to its high narrow windows, the cylindrical drums of its cupolas, and the pilasters that divide up the façade.

30. Ivan the Great, the tallest of the Kremlin buildings and a Moscow landmark. Formerly used as a watch-tower, it was designed by Bon Friazin and built in 1508.

31. *Cathedral of the Assumption (Uspenski Sobor), the oldest cathedral of the Moscow Kremlin. It was built in 1475–79 by the Italian architect Fioravante on the site of an older church of the same name. From the sixteenth century it was the place where tsars were crowned.*

32. *The ikonostasis or altar screen in Orthodox churches serves to conceal the altar and the secret part of the liturgy from the eyes of the laity. The central 'royal doors' are opened for the officiating clergy to emerge at certain points in the service.*

33. *Cathedral of the Archangel Michael (Arkhangelski Sobor) built by Alevisio Novi from Milan (1505–09) on the site of an earlier cathedral. It served as the burial place of the grand princes and tsars. Next to the altar, in the holiest place, is the brass-bound coffin of Ivan the Terrible.*

on account of his numerous progeny, as Big Nest. Like Andrei before him, Vsevolod did much to civilise and embellish his principality and until his death in 1212 effectively dominated the Russian scene. But following his death, yet another savage dispute broke out over the succession, with disastrous results for what remained of Kievan Rus. Again more Russians sought refuge in the forests of the north and north-west.

THE TATAR YOKE

While Russia relapsed once more into chaos, a new and formidable phenomenon had arisen two thousand miles further east in what is now the People's Republic of Mongolia. Half a century or so earlier, in 1154, a son had been born to Yesugei Bagatur, a minor Mongol chieftain. The child, who was given the name of Temuchin, was found at birth to be clutching in his tiny hand a clot of dried blood, an omen which to the soothsayers rightly seemed to bode ill for the future. On reaching years of discretion, Temuchin was to exchange the name originally bestowed on him for the more resounding title of Jenghiz Khan or Ruler of the World.

Jenghiz spent the first fifty years of his life consolidating his position in his own country, a vast land of desert and steppe and rolling prairie. By 1206, he had brought all the tribes of Mongolia under his sway and raised from among them an effective fighting force of a quarter of a million men. With these he now set out to invade the ancient empire of China. Soon his armies stood before the gates of Peking. Having stormed Peking, he next turned westwards again into the vast expanse, part desert, part prairie, of what is now Kazakhstan. There he encountered and decisively defeated the forces of the Khorezmshah, the mighty ruler of Khorezm or Khiva, master at that time not only of most of Central Asia, but of Afghanistan, Persia and northern India. From Kazakhstan Jenghiz went on in 1220 to seize the ancient cities of Samarkand and Bokhara, then, marching southwards to Balkh in Afghanistan, led his armies across the Hindu Kush and in the spring of 1221 mopped up what was left of the Khorezmian forces on the Indus. After a summer spent agreeably

34. *Church of St Barbara, Moscow. This typical example of Russian neo-classicism was built in 1796–1801 by the architect R.R. Kazakov in place of a sixteenth-century church dedicated to the same martyr.*

enough in the northern foothills of the Hindu Kush he returned to Mongolia.

In the meantime, another Mongol army had crossed Persia, reached the southern slopes of the Caucasus mountains and driven deep into the ancient kingdom of Georgia. Returning in greater strength the following year, they utterly defeated the Georgians and went on to overrun the Ukraine and the Crimea, where they wintered. After which, having routed a Russian force sent out to meet them, they too returned to Mongolia. Three years later, in 1226, Jenghiz himself set out once more from Karakorum, his capital, to crush an insurrection in China. It was to be his last campaign. In August 1227, at the age of seventy-two, he died and his body was brought back to Mongolia for burial.

Jenghiz Khan's death did not mark the limit of the Mongol advance. For his sons and grandsons the next thirty years were to be a period of both consolidation and expansion. 'They made up their mind,' wrote the Venetian traveller, Marco Polo, who reached Mongolia at this time, 'to conquer the entire world.' Jenghiz was now succeeded as great khan by his third son, Ogetai, who ruled over Mongolia itself and much of China. His second son, Chagatai, inherited the greater part of Turkestan. To his fourth son, Tolui, went his household and treasury, the ancestral territories and pastures, and the seasoned core of shock troops that formed the main striking force of the Mongol armies. Finally, to his grandson, Batu, fell the Golden Horde, whose vast territories now included most of Siberia and Kazakhstan, and reached as far as the frontiers of European Russia. In the years that followed, Jenghiz's successors were further to consolidate their hold on Persia, Central Asia and the Caucasus, and to conquer all China north of the Yangtse.

The Mongols' initial advance into Russia proved in the event to have been no more than a reconnaissance. Their return ten years later came as a shock to the Russians, who found them frightening to behold, 'with thin hair upon their upper lips and in the pit of their chins, light and nimble bodies with short legs as though made for riding a horse . . . Their speech is sudden and loud, coming as it were from a hollowed throat.'

Between 1237 and 1242 Batu, gathering his strength, struck far into Russia itself and beyond Russia into Poland and Hungary. One town after another fell to the invaders. Hurling his horsemen across the Volga in December 1237, he stormed first Riazan, then Kolomna, then Moscow, then Suzdal and Vladimir. In the spring of 1238 he turned northwards against Novgorod, but then, held up by its marshy approaches, withdrew. In 1240, swinging south again, he stormed and utterly destroyed Kiev itself. Next, crossing the Carpathians, he overran Poland and Hungary. Two years later the Mongol Empire reached from Peking to the gates of Vienna.

But now the news reached Batu that his uncle, the Great Khan Ogetai, had died, and he at once set out for Karakorum to help choose a successor. By the time he returned from this journey, his army's advance had lost its initial impetus. Consolidating his position, he set up his headquarters at Sarai on the lower Volga, which for the next two centuries was to serve as capital of the Golden Horde.

By the middle of the thirteenth century, almost the whole of European Russia had fallen under Mongol suzerainty. The Mongols did little to disturb their vassals' way of life, leaving the Russian princes to rule over their own principalities and collect their own taxes, provided always that they paid tribute and did homage to their Mongol masters.

Profiting by the Mongol conquest, the Russians' northern enemies had been quick to take advantage of their misfortunes, the Swedes seizing Finland, the Danes part of what is now Estonia, and the Teutonic Knights, a crusading order who had moved there from Germany, the lands that lay near the mouth of the Western Dvina and the Niemen. Meanwhile, further south, Vsevolod Big Nest's son Yaroslav, who succeeded his father in 1212, had rebuilt what remained of Suzdal, while in northern Russia Yaroslav's exceptionally able son Alexander became ruler of the ancient city state of Novgorod. Though Novgorod had never been conquered by the Mongols, Prince Alexander wisely chose to pay them tribute, thus leaving himself free to face the enemies who threatened him from the north and west. In 1240 he defeated the Swedes in a memorable battle on the Neva, thus winning for himself the resounding title of Alexander Nevski or Alexander of the Neva. The Teutonic Knights he destroyed no less decisively in a savage encounter on the frozen expanse of Lake Peipus. Following his father Yaroslav's death in 1252, Alexander Nevski succeeded him as grand prince of Vladimir. In 1263 he too died and was buried at Vladimir. In a score of years he helped restore Russian confidence and became a Russian national hero, being in due course canonised by the Russian Orthodox Church.

The Russians were to spend the next two and a half centuries under Mongol rule. The enduring effect of this on their national character and subsequent evolution and development was considerable. Though, thanks very largely to the Orthodox Church, they somehow managed to preserve their sense of nationhood, they were from the middle of the thirteenth century cut off from the civilising influences of western Europe and directly exposed to the Mongol concept of a strongly centralised and regimented autocracy, with significant consequences for their eventual political development.

One important outcome of these years was the gradual rise of the little township of Moscow, founded a century earlier by Yuri Dolgoruki, to be the chief repository of power in Russia. From a lonely fortress, by the second half of the thirteenth century Moscow or Muscovy had become an independent principality, whose territories with the years steadily increased in extent. In 1328 Prince Ivan Kalita or John the Moneybag of Muscovy (thus known for his effectiveness as a collector of taxes) was officially recognised by his Mongol suzerains as grand prince and tax collector in chief. Before long Muscovy had completely swallowed up the principality of Vladimir, of which it had once been part, and had at the same time become the seat of the Orthodox metropolitan. With time, too, the titles of both grand prince and metropolitan came to include the significant words *Vseya Rusi:* 'Of All Russia'. From the earliest times a close connection between Church and State was an essential feature of the Russian system of government, and over the centuries successive church leaders played a decisive part in the nation's affairs.

In their prayers the Russian princes had long implored the Almighty to 'take away the Tartars', begging that 'the Candle', in other words, was what was left of Russia's national spirit, 'should not be extinguished'. For a hundred years and more their prayers remained unanswered. Then, towards the end of the fourteenth century, fighting broke out all at once between rival Tatar factions and, seizing their opportunity, the Russians joined in. On 8 September 1380, after the famous Saint Sergei of Radonezh had blessed his troops, Grand Prince Dmitri of Muscovy, thereafter to be known as Dmitri Donskoi or Dmitri of the Don, boldly engaged the Khan of the Golden Horde in battle at Kulikovo on the marshy right bank of the Don, and heavily defeated him. But the Tatars had not yet been taken away; on the contrary, they were still very much there, waiting for an early chance to avenge their defeat. However, after a century and a half, the legend of their invincibility had been undermined, Russian morale had been restored, and Moscow's claim to the leadership of all Russia strongly and effectively asserted. Even so, the years that followed were difficult ones for the Russians. Though the power of the Golden Horde had begun to decline, their Tatar suzerains continued to tax and harass them. Moreover, following the marriage of Queen Hedwig (Jadwiga) of Poland with Prince Jagiello of Lithuania and the dynastic union of their two countries in 1385, a powerful new Roman Catholic, and potentially hostile, Polish-Lithuanian state had emerged on their western borders.

Cathedral of St Basil the Blessed, Moscow. Lithograph.

44

THE TABLES TURNED

In 1462, following the death of his father, Prince Vasili, began the long and eventful reign of Ivan III of Muscovy, to be known to history, with good reason, as Ivan the Great. During his forty-three years as grand prince, Ivan – able, ruthless and of striking appearance – more than trebled the extent of his dominions, vastly increased his country's standing and prestige, and won for himself the well-deserved title of 'Assembler of Russia'. Overrunning Novgorod and Pskov, Rostov, Riazan and Yaroslavl, he quickly made himself master of most of northern Russia. The Tatar khans he did not directly confront, but skilfully played off one against the other, until, without ever fighting a battle against them, he had, in effect, freed Russia from the Tatar yoke. The other Russian princes soon came to accept his primacy. Almost imperceptibly Muscovy had become the biggest country in Europe. But when, from his capital in the West, the Holy Roman Emperor condescendingly offered Ivan the title of king, the latter abruptly declined it. He had other plans in mind.

Early in his reign Ivan had married Sophia Paleologue, the bulky niece of the last Emperor of Byzantium, assuming at the same time as his coat of arms the double-headed eagle of the Eastern Empire. If Byzantium, now fallen to the Turks, had been the Second Rome, might not Moscow become the Third? Increasingly, the title tsar, derived from the Latin caesar, was now used to designate the grand prince of Muscovy. Increasingly, too, Ivan began to surround himself with trappings of imperial power. Bringing to Moscow a succession of Greek and Italian architects, he set himself to make it a worthy capital for an empire. More than a century earlier four stone cathedrals had been built within the Kremlin's wooden walls, symbolising yet again the strong and enduring links between Church and State, while in the days of Dmitri Donskoi a stone wall had replaced the Kremlin's wooden fortifications. Now, under Ivan, walls, cathedrals and palaces all took on a new magnificence.

Ivan the Great died in 1506 and was succeeded by his son Vasili, who enjoyed power at least as much as his father had done. 'He holds,' wrote Baron von Herberstein, Ambassador of the Holy Roman Empire in Moscow, 'total control over the lives and property of every one of his subjects.' On Vasili's death in 1533 he was succeeded by his three-year-old son Ivan, fourth of that name, later to be known, with every justification, as *Grosni,* the Terrible.

The early years of the new reign were chaotic. With the autocracy in suspense, the great nobles or boyars plotted and fought among themselves. But, on attaining the age of fourteen, Ivan, a more formidable character than his subjects had yet realised, took charge himself. Immediately, the most troublesome of the nobles, Prince Andrei Shuiski, was summarily condemned to death and executed. Three years later Ivan had himself crowned Tsar of All Russia. A notable reign had begun.

Having assumed supreme power, Ivan's next step was to raise a standing army. Backed by this, in 1552, reversing the roles, he first stormed the great Tatar stronghold of Kazan on the Upper Volga. Four years later he captured the Tatar port of Astrakhan at the mouth of the Volga, which gave him effective control of that river as far as the Caspian. To celebrate his triumph over the Tatars, he built on the Red Square in Moscow the altogether fantastic Church of St Basil the Blessed, of late duly resanctified, like the Kremlin churches, for use as an Orthodox cathedral.

By his initial victories over the Tatars, Ivan had opened up vast regions to Russian colonisation, in particular Siberia, long under loose Tatar dominion. In 1558, pursuing his early advantage, he empowered Grigori Stroganov, a merchant-adventurer from Novgorod, to establish a first trading post on the Upper Kama River. A score of years later, the Cossack Hetman Yermak set out with Moscow's blessing, and a force of eight hundred and forty Cossacks, to conquer fresh territories beyond the Urals. This marked the beginning of a process that was to continue, with scarcely an interruption, for the next three hundred years and more.

It is thus that in Ivan's day we first become aware of that very Russian phenomenon, the Cossacks, their name being derived from a Tatar word signifying horseman or rebel. For the most part ethnic Russians who preferred the freebooting life of frontiersmen to a more sedentary existence elsewhere, the Cossacks had over the years gravitated to the steppes of Russia's southern and eastern borders, where in a haphazard way they periodically skirmished, but also interbred, with their Tatar neighbours. Grouping themselves in time into armed bands, each under its own atman or hetman, they eventually developed into a kind of irregular frontier force, not always entirely under control.

Looking northwards and westwards, it became another of Ivan's chief aims to break through to the Baltic. In 1558 he had, with some measure of success, attacked the Teutonic Knights, the weakest of his western neighbours. But in Sweden and Lithuania-Poland he found more formidable adversaries, and the Northern War which now began was to drag on inconclusively for a score of years. In the end he was forced to abandon the parts of Lithuania he had originally occupied, while the Swedes annexed Estonia and took back the strip of territory which the Russians had won from them on the Gulf of Finland. Despite all his efforts, Ivan's strategically far-sighted attempt to gain a foothold on the Baltic had failed.

In 1560 Ivan's wife Anastasia died – of poison he was convinced. His character now seemed to change for the worse. His pent-up wrath he vented on the boyars. Declaring that he was renouncing the throne on account of the treachery which surrounded him, he only agreed to reconsider this dramatic decision on his own terms. The traitors, he said, must be punished. To handle this, he would set up his own *Oprichnina* or secret police. Soon the *Oprichnina* became a state within a state. Another typically Russian institution had been established. Clothed from head to foot in black, mounted on black horses and carrying a severed dog's head at their saddle-bows, the *Oprichniki* brought terror wherever they went, utterly destroying, for example, Moscow's principal rival, the ancient city of Novgorod, and massacring some sixty thousand of its inhabitants out of hand on grounds of suspected disloyalty. In his own rather curious way, however, Ivan remained a deeply religious man, being careful, after each bout of executions, to send to the monasteries lists of his victims so that the monks might pray for their souls. At Alexandrovsk, outside Moscow, he set up a monastery of his own, where in the role of abbot he himself presided over weird religious rites.

Ivan died in 1584. He must rank as one of the handful of revolutionary leaders who over the centuries left their mark on Russia and each in his own way changed the course of Russian history. By deliberately building up a strong class of *pomeshchiki* or serving gentry, he provided a counter-balance to the great nobles and laid the foundations of a centralised autocracy under which each class of the population was bound to the state by bonds of compulsory service. By restricting the peasants' freedom of movement, he also took a significant step in the direction of establishing serfdom, while with the *Oprichniki* he set the precedent for an effective and ubiquitous force of security police. At the same time, by confronting the

Novodevichi Convent, Moscow. Lithograph.

35. Gur Emir, Samarkand, burial place of Timur (Tamerlane) and his heirs, built in 1405.

Tatars and despatching Grigori Stroganov and Yermak to Siberia, he opened up immense regions to future Russian expansion. Though in the end he failed to force his way through to the Baltic, he gave active encouragement to merchants from the West and thereby prepared the way for closer relations with western Europe. But by his own excesses Ivan destroyed much of what he had himself created: his standing army, his country's prosperity and, finally, by a well-aimed blow from his steel-pointed staff, his own eldest son, leaving Russia to be ruled over after his death by his feeble-minded second son Fyodor.

Fyodor was to be tsar in name only. On Ivan's death, power passed to Fyodor's astute brother-in-law, Boris Godunov, a minor boyar of Tatar origin, who, after winning the old Tsar's confidence, married off his sister to Fyodor and, having established valuable connections with the *Oprichniki,* succeeded, after Ivan's death, in having himself declared regent.

TIME OF TROUBLES

36. Taki Zagaron ('Jewellers' Dome') in the old merchant quarter of Bokhara. Built in the fifteenth century at the junction of two streets, it serves as the focal point around which cluster many smaller domes covering innumerable little shops of traders and craftsmen. (pp. 50–51)

Boris Godunov proved in the event a more than adequate regent, continuing many of Ivan's policies, though with a sanity and moderation his predecessor had lacked. Like Ivan, he made it his business to build up the landed gentry at the expense of the great nobles, while binding the peasants still closer to the soil. The *Oprichniki* he replaced in due course by a less obtrusive but no less effective security force. In the north, he resumed the war against the Swedes, while at the same time actively continuing the conquest and colonisation of Siberia, whence his own forebears, it was said, had originally hailed. For a time, Russia enjoyed a period of relative quiet and prosperity. When young Tsar Fyodor died in 1598, leaving, so far as anyone knew, no heir, Boris was in due course elected tsar.

Late in life Ivan the Terrible had, it is true, fathered a third son, Dmitri Ivanovich, the child of a seventh and somewhat dubious marriage to a certain Maria Nagaya. But in 1591 little Dmitri had

37. *Taki Sarafon ('Moneychangers'*
Dome'), sixteenth century, Bokhara.
Also built at a street junction in the
bazaar, this is the smallest of the domed
trading areas that were a feature of the
old quarter. Though it lacks the usual
circular galleries within, it is
architecturally impressive with its
massive arcading supporting the dome.

38. *Gur Emir, Samarkand. With its*
fluted turquoise dome on an octagonal
base, this is one of the world's most
beautiful buildings. It was originally
raised by Tamerlane for his beloved
grandson, Mohammed-Sultan, killed in
battle against the Seljuk Turks in 1403.

39. An Uzbek woman with her children in the Ferghana Valley. Traditionally, Uzbek girls were married off by their parents at 13 or 14, often to a relative so as to prevent fragmentation of family land. Despite many changes in recent decades, old customs and attitudes still continue in Uzbekistan.

40. A mother and son in Hamzabad, Uzbekistan. Soviet rule in some ways improved the lot of women in the Central Asian republics, enabling them to escape confinement to the home, obtain an education and take up jobs. Even so, the role of wife and mother remains all-important.

41. Portal of the Ulug Beg Medresseh, Samarkand. One of the three great Moslem colleges around the Registan, the central square of the old city, it was built by Tamerlane's grandson, Ulug Beg, a great scholar and astronomer. He became ruler of the Mongol Empire in 1447 but was murdered by his son two years later. (p. 56)

42. Ulug Beg Medresseh, Samarkand (1417–20). Its design was well suited to its pedagogical purpose: the high-domed halls at each corner were used for lectures, while the rooms on the ground and upper floors around the courtyard were residential. Besides theology, such colleges provided instruction in natural sciences, mathematics, astronomy, philosophy and literature. (p. 57)

43, 44. Samarkand: tiled walls with typical Islamic ornamentation – arabesques, geometrical designs and stylised floral patterns. Since Islam forbade figural representation, these motifs were often supplemented by elaborate calligraphy, usually quotations from the Koran.

45. Hazret Shakh-i-Zindeh (Tomb of the Living King), Samarkand, interior of a memorial chamber attached to the tomb of Kasim Ibn Abbas, a cousin of the Prophet martyred by Christians in the seventh century after converting Sogdiana to Islam. An ancient pilgrimage site, the shrine was begun in 1326 and continued under Timur and Ulug Beg.

46. *Portal of Tillah Kari Medresseh on the Registan, Samarkand. Built on the site of an earlier caravanserai, it serves as both a college and the city's main mosque. At the time of the construction of the mosque (1646–1660), its interior was the most richly gilded and ornamented in all Central Asia.*

47. *Shakh-i-Zindeh, tomb of Kasim Ibn Abbas, Samarkand. The grave of this legendary Moslem saint attracted pilgrims long before Tamerlane's day, when it was embellished with gilded tiles. The Shakh-i-Zindeh, a whole avenue of shrines and tombs dating from the eleventh to twentieth century, is still visited by thousands of the faithful.*

48. *Uzbeks in the Registan, Samarkand.*

49. *Mausoleum of the khans of Shirvan, Shemakha, Azerbaijan. Following the seventh-century Arab conquest of this region, various khanates prospered here. After a period of decline, the khanate of Shirvan (Shemakha) flourished again under Mongol and Persian suzerainty until swallowed up by the Russian Empire in the early nineteenth century.* (pp. 62–63)

died. Some said that his death had been due to an accident with a knife, others, perhaps more convincingly, that he had simply been murdered by Boris Godunov. But of the fact of his death, which his own mother had witnessed, there seemed to be no doubt.

Not, that is, until the year 1603, when, four years after Boris Godunov's accession to the throne, there came the disturbing rumour that little Dmitri had not after all died back in 1591, but was still alive, by now aged twenty-one and at that very moment mustering, with the ready help of the neighbouring King of Poland, an army of Poles and Cossacks with which to march on Moscow and drive Boris from the throne he had usurped. Whereupon, to add to the existing confusion, came the news that Boris Godunov himself had died.

The years that followed were to be known, with every justification, as *Smutnoye Vremya,* a Time of Troubles, in itself a typically Russian phenomenon. Glad to take even a posthumous revenge on Boris Godunov, the great nobles rallied readily to the pretender. The Moscow mob stormed the Kremlin and murdered Boris's widow and son. And a week later the False Dmitri, as he rightly or wrongly came to be known, entered the capital in triumph, clearly convinced of his own authenticity. Quick to welcome him as her son was Maria Nagaya, who fourteen years earlier had herself witnessed little Dmitri's death. It is thus that in Russia, and indeed elsewhere, fact and falsehood sometimes become inextricably mingled.

From the first, the False Dmitri, whose true identity remains a mystery even to historians, showed considerable independence of spirit. Having gained Polish support on the understanding that he would further Polish and Roman Catholic interests in Russia, the first thing he did was to proclaim his loyalty to the Russian Orthodox Church, appoint a new Orthodox patriarch and have himself crowned tsar. But, even so, his Polish connexion and, in particular, his marriage to Maria Mniszech, the beautiful daughter of an impecunious Polish nobleman, were to count against him. Nor did the Muscovites find his manner and behaviour sufficiently regal, complaining that he wore his hat on the side of his head and never, it was said, took an afternoon nap. On the morning of 17 May 1606, the Moscow mob, egged on by a group of discontented nobles led by Prince Vasili Shuiski, stormed the Kremlin and murdered him, later burning his body and firing what remained of it from a cannon in the direction of Poland. After which, Prince Vasili Shuiski was himself proclaimed tsar.

But Tsar Vasili's reign was from the outset dogged by trouble. Hardly had he ascended the throne than a rising broke out, led by one Ivan Bolotnikov, a former galley-slave, who, it soon began to appear, commanded widespread support. Scarcely had this revolt been quelled than a new pretender arose, to be known as the Second False Dmitri and claiming identity not only with Ivan's son, but more particularly with the first False Dmitri, who had been publicly blown from a cannon not many months previously. But his implausibility proved no obstacle to his success. Having, with the ready support of the Poles, assembled a fresh army from the remnants of those led by Bolotnikov and the First False Dmitri, he marched on Moscow and

50. An elderly Uzbek selling green snuff in the bazaar of Rishtan.

boldly besieged the new Tsar in the Kremlin. Moreover, having set up a rival court in the suburbs, he was at once recognised as her deceased husband by the beautiful Maria Mniszech, who promptly joined him there.

Exasperated by his continuing failure to keep order, the citizens of Moscow now turned on Tsar Vasili Shuiski and dethroned him. Again Russia was without a tsar and again chaos prevailed. In despair, the nobles and church authorities now offered the Russian throne to Wladislaw, son of King Sigismund of Poland. But King Sigismund, whose troops, already besieging Smolensk, were by this time also occupying most of Moscow, including the Kremlin, replied that he wanted the throne, not for his son, but for himself, his purpose being, in other words, to make Russia a Polish dependency. By now the Second False Dmitri had been murdered and a third had made his appearance in Pskov.

It was at this stage that a group of patriotic Russians came together to make a stand against the Poles. On Christmas Day 1610, the Patriarch of Moscow issued a proclamation calling on all loyal Russians to rise in their country's defence. A new spirit was abroad. A first attempt to dislodge the Poles from the Kremlin failed, but Russian resistance grew and by the end of 1611 a kind of national militia had come into being, led by Prince Dmitri Pozharski and by a cattle-dealer from Nizhni Novgorod named Kuzma Minin. In July 1612, after first assembling their troops at Yaroslavl on the Volga, the prince and the cattle-dealer marched on Moscow and, following some fierce fighting, secured the surrender of the Polish garrison. Moscow was again in Russian hands, but Russia was still without a tsar.

A score of years earlier, when Boris Godunov had been elected, his principal rival for the throne had been Fyodor Nikitich Romanov, an able minor noble, who had subsequently been relegated to a monastery. Since then Fyodor Nikitich, rising above this earlier setback to his fortunes, had had a successful ecclesiastical career, becoming in due course metropolitan and taking a leading part in national affairs. When, early in 1613, a special Territorial Assembly was summoned to choose a new tsar, few were surprised when Fyodor Nikitich's son, the sixteen-year-old Mikhail Romanov, was unanimously elected. Soon after, the new Tsar's father was elected patriarch and thus became to all intents and purposes co-ruler with his son. There could have been no clearer example of the closeness of Church and State.

The Russia over which Mikhail Romanov was to rule for the next thirty years and more was in an appalling state. Most of the towns had been sacked, the countryside laid waste and the population reduced by slaughter, starvation and disease from fourteen millions to nine. Armed bands roamed everywhere. The smaller landowners were a relatively stable element, but it was some time before order could be restored and a peaceful settlement arrived at with the Poles.

In 1645 Mikhail Romanov was succeeded by his somewhat ineffectual son, Alexis the Gentle. From start to finish Alexis's reign was a disturbed one. Even the Orthodox Church was split by a schism which has endured to this day. There was trouble, too, between Russia and Poland in the *Ukraina* or Borderland, an area roughly corresponding to the Ukraine of today. Most of it, including Kiev, the present capital, had for a number of years been part of Poland and the substantial Russian Orthodox population had been under strong and sometimes successful pressure from their Polish masters to turn Roman Catholic. In their hetman, Bogdan Khelmnitzki, the Ukrainian Cossacks, who resented this, found an outstanding leader, under whose command they succeeded in routing three Polish armies. By now master of the Ukraine, Khelmnitzki turned for help to Tsar Alexis, who, proclaiming himself ruler of the Ukraine, declared war on Poland. But after Bogdan's death in 1657, the Ukrainians, finding themselves no more independent under Russian than under Polish rule, rose against the Russians, some of them even enlisting Polish support. The three-cornered conflict which followed lasted fourteen years, during which the whole once fertile region was laid waste. In the end Russians and Poles made peace and dreams of an independent Ukraine faded, though only for the time being. In the meanwhile, the balance of power between Russia and Poland had shifted markedly in Russia's favour.

For Alexis the Gentle there was, however, more trouble in store. In 1669 a band of Cossacks from the Don under the inspired leadership of a certain Stenka Razin launched an insurrection against what they called the oppressors of the Russian people. It was surprisingly successful. Town after town fell to the insurgents. Within a year Moscow itself was threatened. Only now did the Government raise an effective force of foreign-trained troops to meet the threat they presented. Thanks to these, the tide was in the end turned. Stenka, betrayed by his own followers, was captured, taken to Moscow and quartered alive at the Place of the Skull on Red Square. Alexis the Gentle died in 1676, leaving as heir his son Fyodor, a partly paralysed boy of fourteen. Next in the line of succession came Fyodor's short-sighted and mentally deficient brother, Ivan, and finally Peter, aged four, the lively, intelligent child of Alexis's second marriage to the beautiful Natalya Narishkina.

Miniature of the town of Kholui on a lacquered casket.

PETER THE GREAT

On Fyodor's death six years later, the Narishkins, a powerful patrician family in their own right, having declared Ivan incapable of reigning, promptly proclaimed Peter tsar and his mother Natalya regent. They had, however, left out of account Ivan's hideous but determined elder half-sister Sophia, who, calling out the *Streltsi* or Musketeers, a versatile body of men always ready for action, gave them ten roubles each to march on the Kremlin and massacre any Narishkins they could find. After which Sophia was in her turn declared regent and Ivan and Peter co-tsars.

While Sophia installed herself in the Kremlin with Ivan, Natalya now withdrew with Peter to the neighbouring village of Preobrazhenskoye and bided her time. As it happened, Preobrazhenskoye was within easy reach of *Nemetzkaya Sloboda,* the German or Foreign Settlement. Natalya was enlightened enough not to share the prevailing prejudice against foreigners and, as Peter grew up, he was able to acquire much useful knowledge from the foreign craftsmen and technicians who were their neighbours, while from foreign mercenaries such as General Patrick Gordon from Aberdeen he also gained a sound military grounding which was to serve him well in later life.

In August 1689, when Peter was seventeen, the news reached his supporters that his half-sister Sophia was plotting to do away with him and declare herself Autocrat. Dragged from his bed in the middle of the night, Peter was rushed to the nearby Monastery of the Trinity and St Sergei at Sergievo (now Zagorsk), where he was quickly joined by a number of leading nobles and clergy and by a sizeable force of loyal troops. After consigning his sister to the Convent of Novodevichi on the outskirts of Moscow, he next ordered the arrest and execution of as many of her supporters as he could lay hands on. Though his half-brother Ivan did not die for another seven years, Peter, by now a formidable giant of a man, was already tsar in fact as well as in name.

Peter, whose military education had not been wasted on him, spent the next five years strengthening his country's defences. In 1695 the outbreak of war with his neighbour the Sultan of Turkey gave him a welcome chance to try his skill as a military commander. It also caused him to look eastwards, to the Caucasus and the lands beyond the Caspian and the promise they clearly held for Russia. Peter's first move was to lay siege to the Turkish port of Azov on the Black Sea. But the Turkish garrison, still able to receive supplies by sea, held out for month after month. Convinced of Russia's need for more ships, he spent the winter of 1695 collecting a fleet. With this he sailed down the Don and blockaded Azov, which almost at once fell to the Russians.

Russia was once more on the move. Henceforth the creation of a strong navy became one of Peter's foremost aims. More shipyards were built and more foreign experts imported. In his search for fresh skills the Tsar himself led a special embassy to half a dozen European countries, bringing back with him any number of new ideas from the West. But at heart he remained an out-and-out Russian. 'We shall need Europe for a few decades,' was his characteristic comment. 'Then we can turn our backside to her . . .'

While visiting Vienna in the autumn of 1698, Peter received the news that back in Moscow the *Streltsi* had again mutinied. Hurrying back, he at once had a couple of thousand of them executed, himself lending the executioners a ready hand with their grisly and demanding task. It was not long before it became clear that the trouble had yet again originated with his sister Sophia. This time he had her still more closely confined, with three dead *Streltsi* dangling outside her window as a warning. Then, with characteristic enthusiasm, he started to put into effect some of the contemporary ideas he had brought back from Europe, forcing his courtiers, whether they liked it or not, to cut their long beards and discard their old-fashioned Muscovite kaftans in favour of the latest European fashions from the West.

To Peter it had long been clear, as it had been to Ivan before him, that, while expanding eastwards, Russia must also have an outlet to the West. To achieve this, he had to break through to the Baltic. In his way stood the Swedes under their young King Charles XII. For what he had in mind Peter found ready allies in King Christian of Denmark and King Augustus of Poland. In the summer of 1700, after first making peace with Turkey, he despatched a force of forty thousand men to the Gulf of Finland.

But Charles of Sweden was to prove a more formidable enemy than his adversaries had anticipated. Striking first at Copenhagen, he next turned on the advancing Russians and heavily defeated them at Narva. Peter, for his part, was not deterred by this initial setback. Within weeks he had started to assemble a bigger and better army, and in the autumn of 1702 again assumed the offensive, first capturing the stronghold of Noteborg on the Neva and then, in the spring of 1703, seizing the Swedish fortress of Nyenschanz, where the Neva is joined by the Okhta. Here, on a little island in the Neva, known locally as Hare Island, he laid the foundations of the future Fortress of St Peter and St Paul and of the great new city that was to bear his name. The following year he took Narva, triumphantly avenging his earlier defeat there.

But the threat from Sweden remained. Having first defeated Augustus of Poland, Charles was now directly menacing Moscow. At the same time there was once more unrest among the Cossacks in the Ukraine, where the Ukrainian Hetman Ivan Mazepa, impatient of Russian rule, was known to be intriguing with the Swedes. Waiting till 1708, Charles launched a major offensive. While he himself advanced through Poland with one army in the direction of Smolensk, another, under General Loewenhaupt, marched south to join him with further supplies and reinforcements. But, instead of directly attacking Smolensk, Charles for some reason turned south into the Ukraine. This gave Peter his chance. Attacking General Loewenhaupt before he could join forces with the King, he succeeded in capturing the entire Swedish baggage train. Meanwhile, another Russian army under Peter's favourite, Prince Menshikov, had attacked Mazepa and nipped his intended uprising in the bud.

It was thus that, with winter coming on, the Swedish King, hundreds of miles from home, suddenly found himself surrounded by Peter's armies. Having failed to break out in the direction of Moscow, he laid siege in the spring of 1709 to the Russian fortress of Poltava, some two hundred miles south-east of Kiev. It was a bold counter move, but in the event the Russian garrison managed to hold out until in early June Peter's relieving force reached Poltava and inflicted what was to prove a decisive defeat on the besieging force.

Peter's victory over the Swedes at Poltava marked a new phase in Russian history. By it, Russia had become a major military power and firmly established her supremacy in north-eastern Europe. By breaking through to the Baltic, Peter had given her, as he put it, 'a window on the West'. 'The final stone,' he now declared triumphantly, 'has been added to the foundation of St Petersburg.' For him, the city of St Petersburg, new and magnificent, built on the marshy banks of the Neva at enormous cost in human lives and

The Menshikov Palace (nearest) on the Neva, St Petersburg. Lithograph.

treasure, symbolised better than anything the true extent of his achievement. In 1712 he made it the chief city of his empire, a fitting capital for the newest of European great powers. Symbolically, he brought there from Vladimir the remains of Alexander Nevski and reinterred them in a fine new monastery which he dedicated to his memory.

The war with Sweden was to drag on for a dozen years after Poltava until eventually brought to a victorious conclusion in 1721 by the Treaty of Nystad. Under this, Russia, while surrendering Finland, acquired from the Swedes Ingria and part of Karelia as well as the Baltic coast from Riga to Viborg, including most of what is now Latvia and Estonia, and thus established a still firmer foothold on the Baltic. Russia's newly-acquired Baltic provinces were now divided into the three Governments of Estonia, Livonia and Kurland respectively. Lithuania, for the time being, remained part of Poland.

But Peter's dreams of empire were not confined to the Baltic. Like Ivan the Terrible before him, he, too, felt the lure of the East. Fifteen hundred miles away on the outer fringes of his empire, Central Asia and Transcaucasia offered tempting targets for conquest and expansion. And beyond them lay the fabled riches of India. By the beginning of the eighteenth century, Russia had already established a loose suzerainty over the nomad khans who ruled over the Kazakh and Kirghiz tribes of southern Siberia and what is now northern Kazakhstan. Peter now despatched a number of expeditions across the Transcaspian wastes to invade Turkestan. They met in the main with disaster. Indeed, in 1716 the unfortunate leader of one of them, Prince Bekovich-Cherkasski, himself of Tatar origin, was flayed alive and his skin, stuffed with straw, hung above the main gate of Khiva, after which further attempts to invade the emirate of Khiva were, for the time being, abandoned.

On the western shores of the Caspian, then under loose Persian suzerainty, Peter was more successful. In 1722 he succeeded in capturing the ancient and strategically important city of Derbent and in further strengthening the defensive line of Cossack settlements and garrisons reaching across the northern Caucasus from the Black Sea to the Caspian, which roughly followed the course of the River Terek and came to be known as the Great Cossack Line. Further south his forces managed the following year to occupy the city of Baku, 'the key', as Peter put it, 'to all our business'.

By this time deservedly styled 'the Great', 'Pater Patriae' and Emperor of All Russia, Peter died in January 1725 at the age of fifty-two. For thirty years, while relentlessly driving through a succession of radical reforms and forcing every one of his subjects, from the greatest noble to the humblest serf, into the service of the State, he had kept Russia continuously at war and substantially increased the extent of her dominions. For Russia, as the old Muscovy was now officially renamed, his reign was to mark a watershed between the Middle Ages and modern times. It was perhaps only natural that two hundred years later Josip Vissarionovich Stalin, recognising a kindred spirit, should have hailed him as the First Bolshevik.

BOUNDS OF EMPIRE

Peter the Great's only son, Aleksei, had died under torture in the Fortress of St Peter and St Paul, sent there by his father on suspicion of treachery. For a couple of years after Peter's death the imperial throne was occupied by his widow, Catherine. A former servant-girl from the Baltic, who swore and drank and rode like a man, she had been placed there by the Imperial Guards and by her erstwhile lover Prince Menshikov, a one-time pastry-cook and for many years a favourite and boon companion of Peter's. When she died in 1727, Catherine was succeeded by Peter's twelve-year-old grandson Peter Alekseyevich, who was, however, quickly carried off by the smallpox. Again the Imperial Guards intervened, putting in his place Peter's coarse-fibred niece Anna, widow of the Duke of Kurland. With her, Anna brought from the duchy of Kurland a horde of Baltic German advisers, many of them descendants of the old Teutonic Knights, who for the next decade showed themselves as ready to run Russia as they were to run her Baltic provinces, while their imperial mistress gave herself up no less readily to the unbridled pursuit of pleasure. On her death in 1740, Anna was briefly succeeded by her three-month-old great nephew Ivan. But Ivan was in his turn quickly swept away by the Imperial Guards and replaced by Peter the Great's younger daughter, Elizabeth.

Not greatly interested in politics, the new Empress much preferred the company of good-looking young men and the building of magnificent palaces. Her reign was nevertheless marked by a significant shift in Russian foreign policy. French influence replaced German, and in the Seven Years' War Russia, taking the offensive against Prussia, succeeded in occupying Berlin. But in 1761 Elizabeth died and there was yet another change in Russian policy. Her successor was her nephew Karl-Peter-Ulrich, Duke of Holstein, who was now proclaimed tsar as Peter III. Himself a German and a fanatical admirer of all things German, Peter at once made peace with Prussia, most fortunately for this country's King Frederick the Great, who, with the Russians occupying Berlin, had been facing imminent disaster.

Of far greater significance than Peter, however, was his bride, the former Princess Sophia Augusta of Anhalt-Zerbst, who on her reception into the Russian Orthodox Church had been rebaptised Catherine. A pure German, highly intelligent, highly sexed and possessed of immense energy and determination, Catherine rapidly transformed herself into an enthusiastic Russian. By contrast with his wife, Peter was a poor creature. Soon a plot was hatched by Catherine's latest lover, Grigori Orlov, with the support, once again, of the

Imperial Guards, to put her on the throne in his place. On a fine summer's day in 1762 Catherine, resplendent in military uniform and with two guards regiments as escort, rode into the capital and was proclaimed empress. Having duly abdicated, Peter was quietly murdered a couple of days later.

Catherine, who, at the age of thirty-six, now became Empress of All Russia, was by any standards an exceptional woman, possessing, among numerous other qualities, considerable political acumen. During the thirty-four years of her reign she was to bring Russia greater territorial gains than any sovereign since Ivan the Terrible. Russia's old neighbour and enemy Poland, greatly weakened by internal dissension, offered at this time a tempting and worthwhile target for her ambitions. Sending, on one pretext or another, a military force to Warsaw, she set up in 1768 what was in effect a protectorate over that unfortunate country. It was at this stage that the French, for reasons of their own, encouraged the Sultan of Turkey, who still possessed a common frontier with Poland, to declare war on Russia.

For Catherine, who, like Peter the Great before her, had long had designs on Turkey's European possessions, the ensuing war, which was to last for five years and be fought on several fronts, was entirely welcome. It began, as she had hoped, with a series of Russian victories. By the autumn of 1769, one Russian army had reached the Balkans; the following summer a Russian fleet destroyed the Turkish fleet in the Bay of Chesme, while a second Russian army seized the Crimea.

Another theatre of war was the Caucasus, the massive mountain barrier dividing Europe from Asia which reaches from the Black Sea to the Caspian and, beyond it, the smiling land of Georgia. One of the reasons for Turkey's declaration of war had been Russia's decision to build, as part of the Great Cossack Line, a fort at Mozdok on the River Terek in the northern Caucasus, a move which provoked not only the local tribesmen, but their august protector, the Sultan of Turkey. In the summer of 1769 General von Todtleben, a German officer in the Russian service, having himself crossed the main range of the Caucasus from north to south with a force of four hundred men and four guns, took Tbilisi, capital of the ancient Christian kingdom of Georgia, then in Turkish hands. After which, having received additional reinforcements, he marched on into western Georgia, routed a Turkish army of twelve thousand men and captured the historic city of Kutaisi or Colchis, until then likewise under Turkish occupation.

For the past couple of centuries the Georgians, lacking effective means to preserve their independence, had in practice lived under alternating Turkish or Persian suzerainty, their rulers, though kings in name, being in practice little more than satraps of the Sultan or the Shah. To them the Russian intervention was welcome. But Catherine, having, thanks to General von Todtleben, gained a foothold in Georgia, now decided to withdraw her force from Transcaucasia and consolidate again to the north of the mountains on the Great Cossack Line along the Terek. In 1774, however, the Sultan, by the Treaty of Kutchuk Kainardji, which brought hostilities with

Turkey to a close, formally recognised the Tsar's interest in his numerous Christian subjects, thus providing Russia with a perennial pretext for intervention on their behalf in Transcaucasia or elsewhere. At the same time, the treaty gave the Russians a firm hold on the northern shores of the Black Sea. On these freshly conquered Turkish territories, which included vast areas of the fertile Black Sea steppe, today part of the Ukraine, Catherine bestowed the name of New Russia, at the same time appointing her one-time lover, Prince Grigori Potyomkin, to be their viceroy.

Soon the Empress, encouraged by her victories, was seriously thinking of creating for herself, at Turkey's expense, a new Byzantine Empire, with Constantinople or Tsarigrad, the Imperial City, as its capital. With this as her ultimate aim, she set out early in 1787 on a triumphal state visit to the territories of the New Russia and to Grigori Potyomkin, their viceroy. With her travelled her ally, the Emperor Joseph II of Austria, and Stanislas Poniatowski, another of her former lovers, since 1763 nominal King of Poland. Not unnaturally the Turks took this combined display of power as an act of deliberate provocation and in September 1788 again declared war on both Russia and Austria.

Catherine had hoped that her armies would now sweep unhindered through the Balkans to Constantinople. But, in the event, Turkish resistance proved tougher than had been expected. Only when the great General Suvorov himself took command did things go better. In 1789 he stormed the Turkish fortress of Hadji Bey on the

The Rossi Pavilion in the Summer Garden, St Petersburg. Lithograph.

74

Black Sea coast. Here a Russian fortress and town were built and given the name of Odessa. But by this time both combatants were exhausted and peace between them was signed at Jassy in January 1792. Under the terms of the Treaty of Jassy, Russia made do with Ochakov, with the Black Sea littoral between the Bug and the Dniester, and with Turkish recognition of her right to the Crimea. For the time being no more was heard of the Empress's grandiose plans for a new Byzantine Empire.

In the meantime, large areas of Poland had been shared out between Russia, Prussia and Austria. In 1793 came a second partition, reducing what was left of Poland to a Russian dependency. It was to be followed four years later by a third, under which Russia received by far the largest share, notably Kurland and Lithuania, thus further extending and completing Peter the Great's breakthrough to the Baltic.

In the Caucasus, the principal threat to Georgia came by now from Persia, and when in 1783 the Shah sought to reimpose his suzerainty on that country, King Irakli or Hercules II of Georgia promptly appealed to Russia for protection. As a first step, the newly-appointed Russian commander in chief for the Caucasus, Count Paul Potyomkin, a cousin of Catherine's lover Grigori, established and garrisoned a fortress at the point near the Darial Gap in the northern Caucasus where the River Terek issues from the mountains, giving it the name of Vladikavkaz, Ruler of the Caucasus. Next he converted the rough track leading southwards across the mountains to Tbilisi into a regular road, soon to become famous as the Georgian Military Highway, and himself led across it a force consisting of two Russian Jaeger battalions and four guns with which to garrison the threatened Georgian capital. Early in 1784 Catherine took King Hercules of Georgia under her protection, at the same time making him her vassal.

But, for all this, it was not long before trouble was again brewing in Transcaucasia. Count Potyomkin's two Jaegar battalions were in due course withdrawn from Georgia and in 1795 the Persians, taking advantage of this, had again invaded Georgia and occupied Tbilisi, raping and, incidentally, hamstringing such virgins as they found there. To this Catherine's immediate answer was to declare war on Persia and drive out the invading force. It was to be one of her last acts of policy.

Catherine died in 1796. Her reign had marked a significant stage in Russia's continuing rise to greatness. Unlike **Peter the Great**, for whom she had profound admiration, and whose imperial policy she had in a sense continued, Catherine was no revolutionary. By the end of her reign the radical ideas she had once briefly favoured were repugnant to her. The French Revolution had long since disillusioned her on that score. Nor had she found an answer to the prevailing discontent in her own country. A rebellion started on the Ural River in 1773 by Emelian Pugachov, a roving Don Cossack, claiming to be her murdered husband Peter, had quickly assumed alarming proportions. By the spring of 1774, Pugachov had assembled a force of twenty-five thousand men, with which he was soon threatening

Moscow. Not until General Suvorov himself took the field against him at the head of a strong regular force was he finally captured and killed, and his followers massacred or dispersed. Only then had Catherine, at the instance of Grigori Potyomkin, given some thought to the need for a measure of domestic reform and for a more effective system of internal security.

The Cossacks, always a potential source of trouble, were now at long last brought under some kind of military control, the country was divided for administrative purposes into fifty Governments and the nobles were officially recognised as a statutory ruling class. But, by refusing to face up to the fundamental problem of serfdom, Catherine bequeathed to her successors an increasingly menacing heritage, while the growing westernisation of the Imperial Court only served further to deepen the divide between the Russian ruling class and the 'dark masses' of the people, of whom ninety per cent were by this time serfs, to be bought and sold like cattle to the highest bidder.

INTO EUROPE

Mentally unstable and of doubtful paternity, Catherine's only son, Paul, who succeeded her, could scarcely have been less fitted for the formidable task which confronted him. His mother, who frankly disliked him, had sought to exclude him from the throne. His own eldest son, Alexander, he was rightly inclined to distrust. On coming to the throne he showed the hatred he bore his mother by reversing as many of her decisions as possible and by giving the orders for the remains of his murdered father (if Paul was indeed Peter's son), to be disinterred and reburied amid much pomp.

Paul's original aim had been to keep his country out of foreign wars, but by now half of Europe had been overrun by France's revolutionary armies and her First Consul, Napoleon Bonaparte, was threatening Egypt. In the end, with Great Britain and Austria, he joined the Second Coalition and sent a Russian army under General

Suvorov to northern Italy to support the Austrians. Suvorov, by any standards a great general, as usual won battle after battle. But early in 1801 Paul, dissatisfied with the support he had received from his allies, decided to withdraw from the coalition and resume relations with France. A few weeks later he was, with French encouragement, embarking on a grandiose plan to invade British India from the north. Though in this instance nothing came of it, it was a project which, first originating in Peter the Great's day, was to recur at intervals in one form or another throughout the century that was now beginning, and to prove a source of perennial anxiety to the British. Meanwhile, a few weeks earlier, in December 1800, Paul had, at the request of King George XII of Georgia, formally annexed that country, by this time again under threat from Persia.

In the end, the Court and the military grew tired of Paul. With the complicity of his own son, the Tsarevich Alexander, and, it is generally believed, of the British ambassador, a plan was made to eliminate him. On the night of 23 March 1801, the conspirators, conveniently including the commander of the palace guard, came on him in his private apartments and, having half-strangled him with an officer's silk scarf, polished him off with a malachite paper-weight.

Having at the very least connived at his father's assassination, Paul's eldest son now succeeded him as Emperor Alexander I. For reasons not far to seek, he was to go down to history as the Enigmatic Tsar. A firm favourite of his grandmother, Alexander had as a boy enjoyed a liberal education and in the course of it was believed to have absorbed some liberal principles. But, having once come to the throne, he found, like Catherine before him, that these would be difficult to apply without endangering the autocracy. And of that he had no intention.

After a brief respite, the war against Napoleon had been resumed. Not for the first time (nor indeed for the last) the Russians took a little time to decide which side they were on. Finally, in 1805, after a period of non-alignment, Alexander, alarmed by Napoleon's fresh victories, joined Great Britain and Austria in their Third Coalition against France. But, on at length reaching Central Europe, Russia's armies were heavily defeated by Napoleon at Austerlitz. Other defeats followed and such enthusiasm as Alexander had ever felt for the war in the end evaporated. In the summer of 1807, having first withdrawn from the coalition, he met Napoleon at Tilsit. On a raft spectacularly tethered in the middle of the River Niemen, the two emperors concluded an alliance with the avowed object of dividing Europe up between them. And not only Europe. Now or later they revived the idea, already considered under Paul, of a Russian invasion of India.

But the Franco-Russian Alliance was not destined to last. Five years on, in June 1812, Napoleon, not unlike Adolf Hitler in June 1941, simply invaded Russia, treaty or no treaty. Some three months later, after a bloody but indecisive battle at Borodino, he entered Moscow, to find it abandoned. Shortly after, the empty city was set on fire. By now ready, indeed anxious, to make peace, Napoleon could find no one to negotiate with. By this time Alexander was for his part determined not to make peace so long as a single enemy soldier remained on Russian soil. In this he had the wholehearted support of the Russian people. From a quarrel between emperors the war had, in the modern phrase, become a people's war.

Napoleon's nearest base was a thousand miles away. Withdrawal, by now the only course open to him, presented a daunting prospect. Winter was coming on, supplies were short, morale low and the population profoundly hostile. The French began their retreat in October. The Russians harassed them as they went. That year the snows came early and the wounded froze to death or were butchered by angry peasants. By the time he reached the Berezina, Napoleon had lost the greater part of his army. His defeat the following year at Leipzig was, in the long run, to prove decisive.

After leading the Allied advance into France and entering Paris at the head of his troops in March 1814, Alexander had come to regard himself as the liberator not only of his own country, but of Europe, as an instrument, he firmly believed, of the divine will. At the Congress of Vienna he not unnaturally played a leading part, and it was largely at his instance that after their final victory at Waterloo the Allied sovereigns formed a Holy Alliance under which their relations were in future to be governed by 'the supreme law of God the Saviour'. For a start, the rulers of Russia, Austria and Prussia proceeded to a fourth and for the time being final partition of Poland, under which that unfortunate country disappeared altogether.

Enigmatic to the last, Alexander is generally believed to have died at Taganrog on the Sea of Azov in the winter of 1825, though, according to another version, he was smuggled out in a friend's yacht and lived on for another forty years as a hermit in Siberia. In the ordinary way he would have been succeeded as tsar by his brother Constantine. In fact, however, Constantine had earlier renounced his rights in favour of his younger brother, Nicholas, though neither Nicholas nor the officials concerned had been clearly informed of this. It was thus that, on the news of the Tsar's death reaching St Petersburg, a situation of the utmost confusion arose, which was only resolved when on 14 December Nicholas himself, grasping the danger of any further delay, decreed that both the army and civilian population should forthwith take the oath of allegiance to him as tsar.

But already it was too late. The harm had been done. Though Alexander had for his own part made no concessions to liberalism, his reign had been marked by the first stirrings of a hitherto largely suppressed public opinion. For some time groups of liberally inclined young officers and others, some of whom had served in Europe and so been infected by the political ideas then prevalent there, had been meeting secretly to discuss the need for social and political reform. Nicholas was known to be a dyed-in-the-wool reactionary. Constantine, for no very good reason, had the reputation of a liberal. The news that Nicholas rather than Constantine was to succeed to the throne was enough for the conspirators, who had long been awaiting an opportunity to air their views. It now seemed to them that the moment they had been waiting for had arrived. On 14 December, the day on which Nicholas's decree was published, some three thousand soldiers, urged on by their officers, gathered in the Senate Square in St Petersburg and refused to take the oath of allegiance to Nicholas, shouting instead for Constantine and *Konstitutsia,* a Constitution; many of them, it was said, in the belief that Konstitutsia was Constantine's wife.

The situation was a potentially dangerous one. In the end, when the mutineers refused to disperse, Nicholas had them surrounded by loyal troops, after which cavalry and artillery were used against them, leaving large numbers of dead. Numerous arrests were then made. Of those arrested, one hundred and twenty were brought to trial, five executed and a number sent to Siberia. They were to become famous as the Decembrists. 'I think,' wrote the far-sighted British minister of the day, 'that the seeds are sown which one day will produce important consequences.'

BEYOND THE CAUCASUS

The circumstances which attended his accession left Nicholas in no doubt that his principal purpose in life must be to save Russia from revolution. Existing security measures were now further intensified. 'A state of siege,' wrote one observer, 'has become the normal state of society.' But the revolutionary movement persisted nonetheless, as did the intellectual and creative ferment that went with it. This was the age of Pushkin and Lermontov, of Tolstoi, Gogol, Dostoyevski, Turgenev and Chekhov. 'Only when literature ceases to be written,' wrote Nicholas's Minister of Education, 'will I be able to sleep soundly in my bed.'

But, while reinforcing security at home, Nicholas also pressed on energetically with the forward foreign policy pursued by his predecessors. In December 1800, only a few weeks before his assassination, the Emperor Paul's formal annexation of Georgia had marked another important step towards Russia's ultimate conquest of the Caucasus and Transcaucasia. By the end of 1804, the remaining territories of the ancient Georgian monarchy had, after centuries, been successfully reunited under Russian rule, and soon the Tsar's dominions reached from the Black Sea to the Caspian.

By securing a foothold on the Caspian as well as on the Black Sea, Russia had effectively strengthened her position in relation to both Persia and Turkey. By the end of 1806, Derbent and Baku, both relinquished to the Persians by the Empress Anna after their original conquest by Peter the Great, had been retaken, and for the twenty years that followed, fighting had continued spasmodically in the Caucasus and Transcaucasia against the Turks, the Persians and the various mountain tribes protected by one or the other.

On coming to the throne in 1825, Nicholas I had for his part gone out of his way to despatch a goodwill mission to the Shah to announce his accession. But, while the Emperor's envoy was still in Teheran, the wayward Persians invaded Russian territory and laid siege to Baku. The Russian response was an immediate counter-attack. Within weeks the main Persian army had been soundly defeated and the Russians' chief objective now became the capture of the ancient city of Erivan (Yerevan), historically the capital of Christian Armenia, the rock-strewn, mountainous, little country lying to the south of Georgia and at that time divided between Persia and Turkey.

Like their Georgian neighbours, the Armenians had for centuries lived under alien rule. In both countries the national Church, whether Georgian or Armenian, had played a vital part in keeping the national spirit alive. Speaking distinct languages of their own and each possessing a history and a culture stretching back for thousands of years, both Georgians and Armenians were not only ethnically, but above all temperamentally as different as they could well be from the Russians and indeed from each other: the Georgians dashing extroverts with a style entirely of their own, the Armenians dogged and dour, quick thinkers and hard bargainers. But for both the armies of a Christian tsar provided welcome protection against the never-absent threat of encroachment by their fanatically Moslem neighbours.

In October 1827, after much heavy fighting, during which the Katholikos of Armenia steadfastly held aloft his monastery's holiest relic, praying the while for a Russian victory, Erivan and the neighbouring monastery of Holy Echmiadzin finally fell to the victorious Russians under the command of General Prince Paskevich. Tabriz followed soon after, leaving Teheran at their mercy. Early in 1828 the Treaty of Turkmenshai brought hostilities to an end, confirming Russia's possession of the former Persian khanates of Erivan and Nakhichevan.

No more than a month after this, in March 1828, came the news that, following the defeat of Persia, Russia was once more at war with Turkey, and at once Prince Paskevich-Erivanski, as he had now become, turned his attention to yet another formidable task. From Mount Ararat to the Black Sea, the Russian frontier lay open to attack by Turkey, while in the northern Caucasus, Turkey still held a considerable stretch of Black Sea coast. The Turks, too, were

*52, 53. Wayside tavern in
Turkmenistan, on the road between the
modern town of Mari and the ruins of
the ancient city of Merv, a centre of
Islamic scholarship in the twelfth
century, destroyed by the Mongols in
1221.*

54. *Two old Bokharans. While the
younger inhabitants of this historic city
(present population about 200,000) are
mostly employed in industry, notably
cotton milling and metallurgy, the older
generations still engage in centuries-old
crafts such as metalworking, silk
weaving, rug making and embroidery in
gold and silver thread.*

55. *An Uzbek selling pumpkins on
a quiet morning in Bokhara market.*

56. *Market in Kutaisi, Georgia: peasants selling water melons and handcraft products. This ancient city on the Rioni River, mentioned in records as early as the sixth century BC, was once the capital of the Colchidian and Imeret empires.*

57. *A well-supplied market in Ferghana, Uzbekistan, the main city of the fertile Ferghana Valley. Typically, it is the women who do the selling, while the men talk local politics, drive bargains or even arrange marriages. Patriarchal ways die hard in these Moslem regions.*

58. *An Uzbek family in one of the many tea-houses of Kokand, capital of the Ferghana district of the Uzbek Republic. Kokand, centre of a khanate and rival of Bokhara in the early nineteenth century, was captured by the Russians in 1876.* (pp.88–89)

59. *Market in Kutaisi, Georgia. Thanks to its Mediterranean type of climate and fertile soil, the Georgian Black Sea coast region is ideal for growing a wide range of fruit and vegetables.*

60. *A Moscow market. Though the Russian capital, its population approaching nine million, has many open and covered markets, the choice of produce and high prices do not satisfy the average citizen. Basic food supply is still a problem in most large cities, entailing long hours of standing in line.*

61. Market in Bokhara, Uzbekistan. This region is a leading fruit growing area, supplying Moscow and other large cities with fresh and dried fruit and fruit juices.

62. A Turkmen peasant selling red peppers, an essential ingredient of the local cuisine.

63. Melons and water melons for sale in Ferghana, Uzbekistan. The Central Asian republics are the largest producers of melons, also grown along the Volga and in Moldavia, the Urals and Transcaucasia.

64. Kutaisi market. Georgia, with an abundance of tomatoes, peppers and fruit. Peppers (capiscums), originally from South America, are grown in all the warmer regions of the former USSR. (p. 94)

65. Apples and pomegranates on sale in a covered market in Bokhara. The Soviet Union, alongside the USA and France, was the world's foremost producer of apples, but even so can barely satisfy the demands of the huge home market. (pp. 94–95)

better fighters than the Persians. They also had a strong hold on the Moslem mountain tribes of Chechnia and Daghestan.

Paskevich's instructions were to use every means he now could to take the pressure off Russia's other theatre of war, on the Danube. He was likewise directed to secure her frontier in Asia Minor and the Caucasus by seizing the Turkish pashaliks of Kars and Ardahan in southern Transcaucasia, and the fortresses of Anapa and Poti on the Black Sea. All this with a total fighting force of no more than twelve or fifteen thousand men.

Following a brilliant Russian assault, Kars fell after three days' siege. By this time the fortresses of Anapa and Poti had already succumbed to a combined Russian attack from land and sea. To reach Ardahan, the Russians had first to capture the reputedly impregnable fortress of Akhalsikhe. 'You may sooner snatch the moon from the heavens,' ran an old Turkish saying, 'than the crescent from the mosque of Akhalsikhe.' But Akhalsikhe, with its ring of surrounding mountains, fell to Paskevich on 17 August. By the end of the month Ardahan, too, was in Russian hands, and with it the whole pashalik of Bayazid. The Russians were by this time no more than sixty miles from Erzerum, the chief city of eastern Anatolia. 'Your Majesty's flag,' Paskevich reported triumphantly to the Tsar, 'is now flying over the headwaters of the Euphrates.'

The victorious Paskevich postponed the next phase of his campaign until the following summer. In June 1829 he set out for Erzerum and, after a successful approach march through the mountains, routed the Turkish force confronting him. He then pushed on to the city, which in the event capitulated without a fight. In the Balkans, meanwhile, the Russian armies had likewise been victorious, and on 18 September peace was signed between Russia and Turkey at Adrianople. By this time, all Georgia and Armenia, as well as the former Persian provinces which today constitute the republic of Azerbaijan, were safely in Russian hands, to be governed henceforth from Tbilisi by a Russian viceroy. For the Russians it only remained to impose their will on the turbulent mountain tribes of the Caucasus itself, over whom they claimed sovereignty. Which, in the event, was to prove the toughest task of all.

During the past fifty years the Russians had made big territorial gains at the expense of the Ottoman Empire. But their real target remained Constantinople, Tsarigrad, the Imperial City. Like his grandmother Catherine, Nicholas continued to keep his eye firmly fixed on this as the ultimate prize. By a fresh treaty concluded with Turkey in 1883 he explicitly constituted himself guardian of what he pleased to call the Sick Man of Europe. Over the years his attitude became ever more disquieting to Great Britain and France, and when twenty years later, in 1853, Russia again invaded Turkey's Danubian provinces, the British and French fleets promptly made their appearance in the Bosphorus.

The following year both countries entered what was to become known as the Crimean War on Turkey's side, landing a combined expeditionary force in the Crimea in September 1854. The Allied conduct of the ensuing war, which dragged on inconclusively for two

66. *An Uzbek woman with her children. Uzbek families, though still relatively large, are now mostly nuclear rather than extended. Even so, sons still try to live close to their father's home to continue the tradition of mutual aid. Usually it is the youngest son who remains in the family house.*

years, was almost as inept as that of the Russians. Nicholas, for his part, was deeply mortified by the inefficiency and muddle it revealed both in the Russian military machine and in the country as a whole. He died early in 1855 on his narrow camp bed in the Winter Palace, a saddened and embittered man, with the war still in progress.

Nicholas's son, Alexander II, who succeeded him, came to the throne convinced of the urgent need for peace in the Crimea and reform at home, an issue which, for one reason or another, his predecessors had studiously avoided. Once the Treaty of Paris had brought hostilities to an end, the new Tsar devoted all his very considerable energies to tackling it. First and foremost came the problem of serfdom. Under the existing system the vast majority of the population could still be bought and sold like cattle. Alexander took a realistic view. 'It is better,' he said in 1856, 'to abolish serfdom from above than to wait for it to abolish itself from below.' In 1861 an imperial edict put an end to serfdom and allowed some forty million freed peasants to buy individual holdings with the help of state loans. It was a truly revolutionary step.

Meanwhile, for a score of years Russia's struggle against the mountain tribes of the Caucasus had continued unabated. The worst trouble came from the fiercely Moslem tribes of Chechnia and Daghestan in the eastern Caucasus, though in the western Caucasus there was also spasmodic unrest among the Moslem Circassians. In the Imam Shamyl the Chechens had found an inspired military and religious leader. What had started as a rising against a foreign invader soon became a *jihad,* a holy war against the infidel. In May 1831 a strong force of Murids, the pick of Shamyl's Mohammedan shock troops, had mounted an attack on the Russian strongpoint of Vne-zapnaya or Fort Surprise in eastern Chechnia and successfully ambushed the strong Russian force sent to relieve it. It was the first of a seemingly endless succession of such attacks.

Eventually the Russians came to realise the nature and extent of the danger that confronted them. Plan after plan was drawn up, reinforcements after reinforcements despatched to the Caucasus, and new forts built at fresh strategic points. But the years went by and Shamyl, though heavily outnumbered, succeeded time and again in getting the better of the Russian commanders who confronted him and in inflicting ever heavier casualties on them. Year after year, successive, increasingly elaborate Russian offensives were planned and put into execution with the object of pinning Shamyl down and obliterating him and his nucleus of fanatical fighters. But every time he evaded them and, fading back into the forests and mountains of his native land in true guerrilla fashion, re-emerged unexpectedly elsewhere to spread the revolt and harass his opponents. The campaign dragged on without respite and, after twenty-five years of constant fighting, Shamyl remained as strong and resilient as ever and commanded wider and more enthusiastic support than he had done a quarter of a century before.

Coming when it did, the Crimean War had brought home to the Russians in no uncertain fashion the danger of having such an enemy permanently in their rear. In July 1856 Tsar Alexander, realising that this was an unacceptable hazard, sent to the Caucasus a new and outstanding commander in chief, Prince Alexander Baryatinski. Prince Baryatinski brought to the war against Shamyl a fresh and effective strategy. Setting out in the spring of 1857, three strong Russian columns closed in on the Murid heartland, felling and clearing wide strips of forest and building new roads as they advanced. By the end of 1857, one column had occupied Lower Chechnia and the other two had made equally good progress. But, though Shamyl had suffered heavy losses, he still disposed of a considerable force and enjoyed the support of much of the population.

By now the Russians were pressing him harder than ever. Here and there they were beginning to meet with rather less resistance than previously, and some of the tribes were starting to come over to their side. Worst of all, Shamyl was losing a guerrilla's greatest asset – the initiative. In the summer of 1858, apart from a couple of minor diversions, he did nothing to check the Russians' advance. Gradually they closed in on his hitherto impregnable mountain stronghold of Veden. Then, in April 1859, Veden itself fell to the Russians. Again Shamyl himself escaped, this time taking refuge with a few hundred of his followers in the heart of Daghestan on the high mountain plateau of Gounib, a natural stronghold surrounded on all sides by precipitous escarpments. By July, the Russians, closing in on him from every quarter with a force of as many as forty thousand men, were ready for the final phase of the campaign.

On 25 August 1859 their assault went in. The Russian infantry swarmed up the escarpment in their thousands and soon only a handful of the defenders were left alive. In the end Shamyl, not wishing to condemn those with him to certain death, agreed to treat with the enemy and, in return for a promise that his life and those of his companions would be spared, formally surrendered his sword to Prince Baryatinski. The Russians treated their prisoner with generosity. Tsar Alexander received him in the most friendly possible manner. He visited Moscow and St Petersburg and, after spending ten or twelve years in a comfortable house at Kaluga, was in the end allowed to go on a pilgrimage to Mecca, where he died and was buried not far from the tomb of the Prophet. Today Shamyl's exploits against the Russians are still well remembered in what eventually became the Autonomous Republic of Daghestan.

For a few more years the Circassians kept up their resistance in the western Caucasus, but by 1864 they too had been crushed and some six hundred thousand survivors took refuge in Turkey. After more than thirty years of fighting and many thousands of casualties, Russia's conquest of the Caucasus was complete.

In less than a century the Russians had extended their frontiers deep into the Near and Middle East. By now the Black Sea was well on the way to becoming a Russian lake. The borders of Turkey and Persia had been pushed far back into Asia Minor and Transcaspia. The great mountain barrier of the Caucasus had become an unassailable Russian glacis, while, with an assured hold on the western shore of the Caspian, Russia was clearly poised for the next phase in her rise to world power, namely the conquest of Central Asia.

Russia's possessions in the Caucasus and Transcaucasia were ruled over by a viceroy in Tiflis (now Tbilisi), for centuries the capital of Georgia. Though incorporated since 1800 in the Russian Empire, Georgia and the Georgians continued to retain their highly individual character and characteristics. The newly liberated Armenians likewise. Welcoming the Russians as protectors against their Turkish and Persian oppressors, they took full advantage of the scope offered for their talents by the great empire of which they were now part. For Armenians worldwide, their ancient capital city of Erivan and their great cathedral at Holy Echmiadzin, where the Katholikos of all the Armenians had his see, served as a national and spiritual rallying point.

Across the former Persian province of Azerbaijan, the peace treaty with Persia had drawn an arbitrary line along the River Araxes (Araks), leaving as many native Azeris to the south as to the north of it. For the ordinary Moslem Azeri, peasant life on the barren hillsides and in the rather more fertile valleys of Azerbaijan continued much as before on both sides of the line. Meanwhile, further north, in neighbouring Baku, with the discovery of oil, or rather of its economic significance, a great modern city was soon to grow up round the ancient palace of the Shirvan shahs.

INTO ASIA

The Crimean War notwithstanding, the Russians had by no means abandoned their dreams of empire. The Treaty of Paris had, it is true, temporarily checked their advance in the Middle East. But there was, as yet, nothing to prevent them from expanding to their heart's content in Siberia, in the Far East and in Central Asia.

Starting under Ivan the Terrible, Russia's colonisation of the vast expanse of Siberia had been pursued more or less continuously throughout the seventeenth century. In 1604 the town of Tomsk had been built on the River Ob. Not long after, the Russians reached the

River Yenisei, and not long after that, the Lena. In 1639 their first pioneers came to the Sea of Okhotsk, thus establishing a foothold on the Pacific. In 1653 the Cossack Hetman Khabarov, a man of much the same stamp as his predecessor Yermak a century earlier, reached the Amur River, encroaching for the first time on Chinese territory. In the end Khabarov was obliged to withdraw, but under successive tsars control of the Amur remained Russia's ultimate purpose. During the eighteenth and early nineteenth centuries her explorers continued to range far and wide across Siberia. Finally, in 1803, the whole vast region was organised as a single Government with a governor-general residing in the elegant new town of Irkutsk on the shores of Lake Baikal and a total population of around a million, consisting partly of settlers and partly of convicts and political prisoners. In 1847 the appointment as governor-general of Count N. N. Muravyev, who had won fame twenty years earlier as a dashing military commander under Paskevich in the Caucasus, marked the beginning of a new phase. Control of the Amur River and the improved access this would give to the Pacific became Russia's declared aim, vigorously pursued on her behalf by Muravyev. 'It seems natural for Russia,' he wrote in a characteristic despatch, 'if not to own all Asia, at any rate to control the whole Far Eastern coast.'

Although the Crimean War was by then already in progress, first one and then a second Russian expeditionary force set out for the Amur from Chita in 1854 and 1855; the Chinese offered no resistance; halfhearted French and British attempts at intervention failed; and in May 1858 a treaty was signed with the Chinese at Aigun under which the Amur became the frontier between the two countries. Muravyev had meanwhile secured authority for the establishment of an immense new province embracing Kamchatka, the Sea of Okhotsk and the Amur region, to be known as the Maritime Territory. At the junction of the Amur and Ussuri rivers he founded the new town of Khabarovsk, so named in memory of his remote predecessor Khabarov. In 1860 the Treaty of Aigun was formally confirmed; the whole of the Ussuri region and much else besides became Russian. Sailing down the Pacific coast, Muravyev himself picked a suitable site for the future city of Vladivostok, which, with the help of ice-breakers, could be kept open for shipping all the year round. It was not, however, until the turn of the century that the much discussed plan for a trans-Siberian railway finally became a reality, opening up to future development the whole immense area and its still almost untapped natural resources.

Meanwhile, in Central Asia, too, the Russians were by now beginning to extend their dominions. On the west, what we loosely call Central Asia or Turkestan is bounded by the Caspian and on the east by Lake Baikal. To the north lies Siberia, to the south rises the great mountain barrier of the Pamirs and Himalayas. Between these natural limits extends a vast expanse of desert: to the west the Kara Kum or Black Sands; to the east the Kizil Kum or Red Sands. This is traversed by two great rivers, the Oxus or Amu-Darya and the Jaxartes or Syr-Darya, both rising in the high mountains to the south and eventually finding their way into the Aral Sea. Along their valleys, thousands of years ago, civilisation took root and flourished. Here caravans from China and from the Middle East had their staging posts. Here cities were built and, here, side by side with the pastoral life of the nomads, a more sedentary, civilised way of life evolved. When Alexander of Macedon sacked it in 329 BC, Samarkand was already a great and famous city. Over the centuries successive waves of invaders, Huns, Tatars, Turks and Mongols, swept through the length and breadth of the whole region. In the seventh century of our era the Prophet Mohammed launched from his native Arabia the series of conquests which were soon destined to bring much of the known world, including the whole of Central Asia, under Moslem rule.

The thirteenth century was to find the Turkish Khorezmashahs masters in Moslem Central Asia, only to be swept away in their turn by the Mongols. Jenghiz Khan's great empire was followed in the fourteenth century by that of another great conqueror, Tamerlane (Timur), who ruled over it from his capital in Samarkand, where to this day he lies buried beneath the great turquoise-blue dome of the Gur Emir. By the end of the fifteenth century, power in the lands between the Oxus and the Jaxartes had passed to the Turko-Tatar Uzbeks under their leader Mohammed Shaibani, founder of the Shaibanid dynasty, who for a century or more were to rule over this whole region, now known as Uzbekistan. With the years, Samarkand and Bokhara, famous for the fanaticism of their inhabitants and safe behind their barrier of mountains and deserts, became increasingly cut off from the outside world, as did the neighbouring khanates of

The Great Palace at Pushkin (Tsarskoye Selo), near St Petersburg. Engraving.

Khiva and Kokand. Few travellers reached either city from the West and fewer still lived to tell the tale. Further east, tribes of ferocious Turkmen nomads ranged at will over the deserts of Transcaspia, raiding passing caravans and selling the prisoners they took as slaves in the bazaars of Bokhara and Samarkand, a well-fed Russian fetching the equivalent of a pound sterling or more.

Since the early eighteenth century the tsars had maintained a loose suzerainty over the different Kazakh and Kirghiz tribes of southern Siberia, Semirechye and the region of the Syr-Darya or Jaxartes. This they were to follow up during the first half of the nineteenth century by outright annexation. Having established themselves at Vierny (now Alma Ata) at the foot of the Tien Shan Mountains on the borders of Chinese Turkestan, they were by 1854 poised for the conquest of western Turkestan. In 1840 a Russian expedition from Orenburg against the khanate of Khiva had, like Peter the Great's earlier expedition, met with disaster. Their later campaigns were to be better planned. In the early nineteenth century Turkestan was divided into three relatively weak independent states, the emirate of Bokhara and the khanates of Khiva and Kokand, for centuries very largely cut off from the outside world. In 1855 the Russians seized, as a first step, the Kokandi fort of Ak Mechet (later Perovsk) on the Syr-Darya, where they established another firm base. This, with their existing base at Vierny, gave them a convenient jumping-off point for what they now had in mind.

For the next ten years the Tsar's armies were fully occupied in the Crimea and in subduing the unruly tribes of the Caucasus. It was consequently not until the spring of 1864 that operations were

67. Triumphal Arch, Palace Square,
St Petersburg. The magnificent ensemble
of the Palace Square was completed in
the 1820s by the Italian architect Carlo
Rossi, who was commissioned by Tsar
Alexander I to design the huge building
of the Ministry of War on its northern
side, facing the Winter Palace. The
double triumphal arch, surmounted by
a chariot and Winged Victory,
separating the two wings of this building,
commemorates Russia's victory over
Napoleon.

68. The Great Palace (also known as
Catherine's Palace) at Pushkin, formerly
Tsarskoye Selo (Imperial Village), 15
miles south of St Petersburg. Originally it
was a modest hunting lodge built around
1720 for Peter I by his wife, Catherine.
Some 30 years later, their daughter,
Empress Elizabeth, employed the Italian
architect Bartolomeo Rastrelli to
transform it into a sumptuous Baroque
residence. Its pillared façade, 1,000 feet
long, has a splendid pavilion at one end
and a gold-domed church at the other.
(pp. 106–107)

69. Peterhof, perhaps the most
spectacular of all the palaces around the
imperial capital. It was built in the early
eighteenth century as the summer
residence of Peter the Great, who felt
that for prestige purposes he should have
something to rival Versailles. Below the
palace, the famous Grand Cascade
gushes down the hillside into the Gulf of
Finland over a series of terraces marked
by lines of fountains interspersed with
gilded statues. (pp. 108–109)

resumed in Central Asia. In May of that year a Russian column of two thousand, six hundred men set out across the desert from Vierny, while another, one thousand, six hundred strong, started from Perovsk. In June the first of these captured Aulie Ata, while the second seized the town of Yasi or Turkestan. After which, joining forces in September, they together stormed the citadel of Chimkent, routing an enemy force of ten thousand for the loss of only two Russians.

In order to reassure the other great powers, the Russian Government had the previous year explained to them in a carefully phrased circular that all they were doing was adjusting their frontiers. But now, acting on his own initiative, General Cherniayev, the Russian force commander, pressed on and boldly captured the ancient Kokandi city of Tashkent. In the hope of pacifying the British, who, fearful for India, were by this time showing signs of serious concern, Cherniayev was at once recalled (and promoted). But in the spring of 1866 his successor, General Romanovski, following up this initial advantage, first invaded the emirate of Bokhara and next inflicted a decisive defeat on the Khan of Kokand, who readily made peace and acknowledged himself a vassal of the Tsar. The following year saw the appointment of General K. P. von Kaufmann, an officer of German origin and exceptional ability, as governor-general of Turkestan with his headquarters at Tashkent.

The Russian conquest of Central Asia had in fact scarcely begun. In the spring of 1868 General von Kaufmann found, without much difficulty, a fresh pretext for invading the territory of the Emir of Bokhara and, after taking Samarkand, went on to occupy nearby Urgut and Katta Kurgan. A month later he met and routed the Bokharan main force and, under a treaty signed a month after that, the Emir surrendered Samarkand and the surrounding region to the Tsar and agreed that the rest of his country should become a Russian protectorate.

Kaufmann next turned his attention to the more remote khanate of Khiva. Earlier Russian expeditions had been defeated by the waterless deserts with which the oasis was surrounded. This time nothing was left to chance. Kaufman's force of thirteen thousand men was divided into four columns. It set out in May 1873 with Kaufmann himself in command of the main column, which started from Tashkent. Another column started from Orenburg on the fringes of European Russia and two more from Krasnovodsk and Fort Alexandrovski on the eastern shore of the Caspian. The British Government had meanwhile again been fobbed off with the story that the expedition was only being undertaken in retaliation for border raids.

Although the column from Krasnovodsk was obliged to turn back by the heat and by shortage of water, the other three reached their objective as planned. On 10 June the ancient walled city of Khiva fell without a fight and on 12 August a treaty was signed by the Khan of Khiva and General von Kaufmann, under which the former ceded a large part of his territory to the Tsar and placed the rest under Russian protection. Since 1866 the Khan of Kokand had also

70. *Main entrance of the Great Palace at Tsarskoye Selo, now a fair-sized town renamed Pushkin in honour of the great poet, who attended the imperial lycée there. This palace, like others around St Petersburg, then Leningrad, was devastated during the Second World War. Immense funds and efforts were invested for their complete reconstruction according to old plans and drawings.*

71. *Beside the Moika, St Petersburg, the Stroganov Palace in the background. The city, lying on the delta of the Neva, at the head of the Gulf of Finland, is intersected by many rivers, streams and canals, spanned by 370 bridges. The charm of this 'Venice of the North' is enhanced by the ornamental iron railings along the banks of these waterways.*

72. *Pavilion in the grounds of Pavlovsk Palace. At the time of the construction of the palace the surroundings were laid out as one of the earliest English-style parks in Russia. Its designers made excellent use of the beautiful site on the banks of the River Slavyanka, a few miles from Tsarskoye Selo.*

73. *Pavlovsk Palace, the last of the great imperial summer residences to be raised in the environs of St Petersburg. This Palladian palace, designed by the Scottish architect Charles Cameron, was built in the 1780s on an estate presented by Catherine the Great to her son, later Tsar Paul I – hence the name Pavlovsk.*

74. *Central gateway of the Admiralty, topped by its slender golden spire. Constructed on the site of former dockyards beside the Great Neva in the early eighteenth century, the old Admiralty was completely rebuilt by Zakharov a century later. This is really the hub of the city, from which its three main avenues radiate.*

75. Cathedral of St Nicholas (Nikolski Sobor), St Petersburg. Built in the mid-eighteenth century by the noted architect Chevakinski, a pupil of Rastrelli, the church is remarkable for its richness of form and decor.

76. *In front of Nikolski Sobor,*
commonly known as the Sailors'
Church. One of the most popular of the
working churches in St Petersburg, it
always attracts large crowds on feast
days.

77. *A majestic vista down one of the innumerable waterways of St Petersburg.*

78. *The former Stock Excange building on Strelka Point on the Neva, St Petersburg.*

79. *Stroganov Palace, St Petersburg.
One of the finest of the palaces lining the
Nevski Prospekt, it was built in the
1750s for Prince Stroganov by Rastrelli,
at the point where the Nevski meets the
Moika. Architecturally, it is typical of
the patrician residences raised in the new
Russian capital in the mid-eighteenth
century.*

117

80. Classical gateway leading to an inner harbour, part of the Novaya Hollandia (New Holland) shipyards, St Petersburg. It was designed in Catherine the Great's day by Vallin de la Mothe.

81. Statue of the Emperor Paul I in front of Pavlovsk.

82. Palace of A. V. Kikin, built in 1714 in the Smolni district of St Petersburg for one of Peter I's closest associates. After the execution of its owner for high treason in 1718, it was used to house a natural history collection brought from Holland.

83. The Great Hall or Ballroom of the Hermitage, one of the largest of its many splendid chambers.

84. Wall decoration in the Hermitage. The silk wall-coverings, tapestries, reliefs and gilded ornaments that adorn the interior of this great museum complex provide a splendid setting for some of the world's finest art.

85. Bust of Peter I, the Great, in the Hermitage. It was Peter who chose the site of St Petersburg, as his 'window on the West', in 1703, and supervised every aspect of its rapid construction.

86. Portrait of the Shishmarov Sisters, K. P. Briulov, 1839, Russian Museum, St Petersburg.

87. *The Grecian Hall, Pavlovsk, designed by Charles Cameron, one of the most magnificent chambers in this imperial residence.*

88. *Self-portrait, I. E. Repin, 1878, Russian Museum, St Petersburg. One of the greatest of the 19th-century Russian realist painters, Ilya Efimovich Repin (1844–1930) is noted for his portraits (Glinka, Mussorgski, Turgenev, Tolstoi) as well as for social realist works such as 'The Volga Bargemen'.*

*90, 91. Pavlovsk, near Tsarskoye Selo.
The splendid interior decoration of the
palace was entrusted to the architects
Charles Cameron, D. Quarenghi, Carlo
Rossi, A. N. Voronikin, and a number of
eminent Russian and foreign painters
and sculptors.*

92. Gryphons on the Bank Bridge,
St Petersburg, named, like the Theatre
Bridge and others, after important
nearby buildings.

93. Tauride Palace, St Petersburg, built
by Catherine the Great for Prince
Potyomkin, one of her numerous lovers.

94. Convent of the Resurrection at Smolni, St Petersburg, one of the magnificent buildings designed by Bartolomeo Rastrelli for the Empress Elizabeth. Rastrelli (1700–1771) was the leading architect of the widely influential 'Petersburg Baroque' style.

95. *Summer pavilion in the park of the*
Great Palace, Tsarskoye Selo (Pushkin).
Importing architects, artists and
decorators from the West, in the
eighteenth and nineteenth centuries the
rulers of Russia created for themselves
residences modelled on the palaces of
other European monarchs, and even
exceeded these in extravagant luxury.

129

96. *Tallinn, the old quarter of the capital of Estonia. A city of nearly half a million and a major Baltic port, Tallinn has preserved unspoilt its mediaeval core, now only a tiny part of the urban whole. Many fine merchants' houses in the Lower Town recall the age when Tallinn was a Hanseatic city.*

97. *Jesuit Church of St Kasimir, Vilnius, an early example of the Baroque style, which reached Lithuania from Italy. After the republic was incorporated in the USSR, the church was turned into a Museum of Atheism.*

98, 99. Part of the mediaeval quarter of Tallinn, capital of Estonia, smallest of the three Baltic republics, the first parts of the Soviet Union to achieve full international recognition as independent states.

100. Church of St John the Divine, Vilnius, part of the splendid complex of buildings around the main courtyard of Vilnius University, founded in 1579. The present Baroque edifice from the mid-eighteenth century replaced a fourteenth-century church from the time of Lithuania's conversion to Christianity.

101. *Trakai Castle, Lithuania. Once the centre of pagan resistance to Christian German invaders, Trakai, 15 miles west of Vilnius, was formerly the residence of Lithuanian princes.*

102. *Church of St Anne and Monastery Church of SS Bernard and Francis, Vilnius. Both are late Gothic in style, though the latter has Baroque alterations. St Anne's, brick-built in the early sixteenth century, so impresssed Napoleon in 1812 that he wished he could take it with him.*

been a Russian vassal. But the Russians were not loved there, and in 1875 a strong rebel force drove him from his throne and attacked the Russian garrison. On receiving the news, Kaufmann at once marched on Kokand, routed the rebels and reoccupied the main towns. After which he simply annexed the former khanate, restoring to it its ancient name of Ferghana.

For a score of years the Treaty of Paris had brought peace of a kind to the Near East. But here, too, the Russians were again on the move, with their eyes still firmly fixed on Constantinople as the ultimate prize. In 1875 and 1876 the Slavs of Bosnia, Herzegovina and Bulgaria suddenly rose in their thousands against the Turks; thousands of Russian volunteers flocked to join them and in April 1877 Russia, on the crest of a wave of Pan-Slav enthusiasm, once more declared war on Turkey, yet again launching her attack simultaneously through the Balkans and the Caucasus. By February 1878 a Russian army under General Skobelyev stood before Constantinople. Catherine the Great's dream of a new Byzantium seemed about to be realised. But again, on reaching the Dardanelles, the Russians found the British fleet at anchor in the Sea of Marmara. The Eastern Question, as it had come to be called, had reached another climax. In the end, however, the Russians withdrew; war was avoided; and, thanks to the good offices of the German Chancellor and the relative restraint shown by all concerned, a peaceful settlement was finally arrived at.

In Central Asia all that now remained unaccounted for between the frontiers of Russia and those of Persia, Afghanistan and ultimately British India was the desolate region of Transcaspia, inhabited by the ferocious Tekke Turkmen, notorious raiders of caravans and inveterate traders in slaves. In 1879 a first Russian attack on the Turkmen stronghold of Geok Tepe was driven off with heavy losses. But two years later a force of over seven thousand men, commanded by the now famous General Skobelyev, succeeded in storming Geok Tepe and massacring the entire Turkmen population, twenty thousand of whom were killed in one day for a loss of some three hundred Russians. 'The harder you hit them,' remarked Skobelyev characteristically, 'the longer they will stay quiet afterwards.'

On 6 May 1881, the whole of Transcaspia was annexed by Russia. Three years later, in 1884, the Russians followed this up by occupying the nearby strategically situated oasis of Merv, giving the British an attack of what at the time was called 'Mervousness'. Russia's conquest of Central Asia was by now to all intents and purposes complete. In the space of a few years the Tsar's armies had conquered an area the size of all Western Europe. Only a few miles of rock and desert separated the respective spheres of interest of the British and Russian Empires. Briefly, at the turn of the century, an armed clash between them seemed possible, even likely. But there soon came a shift in the European balance of power and a change in the European system of alliances, and in a few years Britain and Russia had become allies.

Just as the viceroyalty of the Caucasus was governed from Tiflis and Siberia from Irkutsk, so Russia's new Central Asian dominions

103. The church at Chesme, half way between Petersburg and Tsarskoye Selo, was built together with the adjoining palace by Catherine the Great in the 'Turkish' manner to celebrate the Russian naval victory over the Turks off Chesme, on the coast of Anatolia, in 1780.

were henceforth ruled over by a Russian governor-general and commander-in-chief with his headquarters in the old Kokandi city of Tashkent. Here a tree-lined avenue neatly divided the cantonments and officers' quarters of the new Russian city from the bazaars and mosques and huddled mud-built houses of the old native town. Further west, the Emir of Bokhara and the Khan of Khiva continued to rule much as they had always done over their somewhat diminished kingdoms, though in the knowledge that they were no more than vassals of the Russian Tsar, whose Asian dominions now reached from the Caspian to the Pacific.

REVOLUTION

At home, despite urgent warnings from all quarters, Alexander II had persisted in his policy of reform. Serfdom had been abolished and millions of former serfs, still constituting the vast majority of the population, had now become peasant proprietors, some of whom, life and human nature being what they are, rose quickly in the social scale, while others continued as hewers of wood and drawers of water. Meanwhile, in the cities the second half of the century had been marked by a measure of industrial development and by the emergence for the first time of what could properly be called an industrial proletariat. Against this changing social background the revolutionary movement, for all the watchfulness of the Tsar's secret police, continued as active as ever. Finally, in March 1881, after several attempts, a terrorist group called the People's Will succeeded in assassinating the Emperor Alexander, just as he was about to sign a proclamation taking a first step in the direction of constitutional government.

The effect was to set back any hope of political reform for another quarter of a century. On succeeding to the throne, Alexander's burly son, Alexander III, at once tore up the proclamation his father had been about to sign. There was no longer any talk of reform and the existing security measures were further tightened. A dozen years later Alexander III died in his bed, having managed to avoid assassination and to keep his country out of war. His son, Nicholas II, who came to the throne in 1894, was to prove less fortunate.

By the year 1900, the population of the Russian Empire, extending as it now did from the Baltic to the Pacific and from the Arctic Ocean to the Afghan border, numbered 128 millions, more than three times as much as a hundred years before. Though the peasants were still in the vast majority, industrial development had by now brought into being a rootless and restless urban proletariat of three millions. In southern Russia and the Ukraine, the number of iron works and coal mines was growing, textile mills were making their appearance in Moscow and St Petersburg, and oil wells and refineries in the Caucasus. Throughout the Empire a network of railways had been created. In Central Asia the Transcaspian line now linked Krasnovodsk with Tashkent. Work on the trans-Siberian line had begun in 1891 and both in Russia and abroad, notably in Western Europe, large sums were being raised to finance the country's industrialisation. At the same time a new class of entrepreneurs and industrialists had emerged. From feudal and patriarchal, Russia was at long last becoming capitalist, and, what is more, accepting this new stage in her development with unexpected alacrity.

In February 1898, as a natural consequence, it might be said, of these developments, the first Marxist party was founded in Russia, the Social Democrats. In 1902 it split into two factions, Mensheviks and Bolsheviks, the latter led by Vladimir Ilich Ulyanov, otherwise known as Lenin. A more immediate threat to the regime were, to all appearances, the openly terrorist Social Revolutionaries. Worried by this renewal of revolutionary activity, Plehve, the Minister of the Interior, gave it as his view that 'a useful little war' might furnish a welcome diversion. Others, including Tsar Nicholas, were inclined to agree with him.

As though in answer to their prayers, the Russo-Japanese War, in itself a consequence of Russia's forward policy in the Far East, began early in 1904, but from the first it went badly for the Russians, and in May 1905 their fleet was wiped out at Tsushima. A treaty of peace, deeply humiliating for Russia, was signed three months later.

Far from providing a useful distraction, the war had made things at home a good deal worse. Plehve himself had been assassinated by the Social Revolutionaries in 1904. And on Sunday, 22 January 1905, not many months after the outbreak of war, a great crowd of workers, carrying ikons and singing hymns, converged on the Winter Palace to petition the Tsar. Just as they had done on the nearby Senate Square eighty years earlier, the troops opened fire on the crowd and a number of people were killed. By nightfall, not surprisingly, the Government were facing a genuinely revolutionary situation.

Serious disturbances continued all over the country throughout 1905. In October a general strike was followed by the formation in St Petersburg of the First Workers' Council or Soviet, led by an able young revolutionary called Bronstein or Trotski. Late in December Tsar Nicholas agreed, under pressure, to the election of a *Duma* or

National Assembly, resembling, to some extent, what his grandfather had had in mind twenty-five years before.

'A war,' said Lenin in 1913, 'would be a very helpful thing for the Revolution.' Twelve months later war broke out. It was to last four long years. The world, thereafter, would never be the same again. 'War,' Trotski once said acutely, 'is the locomotive of history.' From 1914 onwards, the Russians fought, as always, with great courage and endurance. But they were badly led, badly equipped and badly supplied. In three years they lost two million dead.

As Lenin had rightly foreseen, revolutionary ideas now fell on fertile ground. Early in March 1917 a shortage of bread led to disturbances in St Petersburg or Petrograd, as it had been renamed to give it a less German sound. Tens of thousands of workers came out on strike. The Cossacks, when called out in support of the police, failed to respond. On 10 March the Tsar dissolved the *Duma* and a Soviet or Council of Workers and Soldiers was set up in the Tauride Palace in its place. A couple of days later two regiments of the Imperial Guards mutinied and distributed their arms to the crowd. A Provisional Government was formed, and on 15 March the Tsar signed his abdication. The March Revolution, as it came to be known, was over. But there was more to come.

On 16 April 1917, Lenin, returning, with secret German connivance, from exile in Switzerland, arrived at the Finland Station in Petrograd. Climbing onto a conveniently placed armoured car of British manufacture, he declared that what he stood for was peace, bread and freedom. His, he said, would be no bourgeois revolution, but a world-wide socialist proletarian revolution. He promised peace

Mikhail Papenov: Haymaking Season, painting on a lacquered casket, 1947.

negotiations forthwith with the Central Powers, the redistribution of agricultural land, and workers' control of the factories. His programme had broad and immediate appeal. Food and an end to the war was what people wanted most. Bolshevik influence spread fast. Discipline began to break down among the troops at the front. The peasants seized the landlords' estates. The workers took over the factories. All over the country power began to pass to the local soviets which were by now being set up everywhere. In the All-Russian Congress of Soviets, the Bolsheviks were, it is true, still in a minority but, as a political force, Lenin's leadership outweighed any lack of numbers. In July a first Bolshevik attempt at a coup was suppressed by the Provisional Government, and Lenin fled to the relative safety of Finland.

Returning clandestinely to Petrograd in October, he decided this time on armed insurrection. On 7 November Red Guards and mutinous troops under Bolshevik control seized the key points in the capital, including the Winter Palace. Most of the members of the Provisional Government were put under arrest and on 8 November a new Government, known as the Council of People's Commissars, was set up under Lenin's chairmanship. It immediately issued two decrees, the first calling for an early peace, the second abolishing private ownership of land. In Petrograd, the Bolsheviks had won a quick and easy victory. In Moscow, it took several days to establish their authority. In the rest of the country, as can be imagined, uncertainty and confusion prevailed. It was to be resolved over the next four years by a bloody and singularly savage civil war.

On 18 January a Constituent Assembly met in the Tauride Palace. But in Lenin's scheme of things there was no room for what he called 'parliamentary illusions'. Next day the Assembly was dispersed by the Red Guards on duty. Seven months later it was announced that in future sovereign power would be vested in the Congress of Soviets, which, on orders from above, now provided the Russian Soviet Federated Socialist Republic, as the empire of the tsars was henceforward to be called, with a suitable constitution.

At the Finland Station, Lenin had promised peace and, as proof of his good intentions, had opened negotiations with the Central Powers. The terms offered by the Germans and Austrians were so harsh that even the Bolsheviks hesitated to accept them. But in the end, Lenin, fearing for the Revolution if the war went on, threw all his weight on the side of peace at any price, and on 3 March 1918 a treaty was signed at Brest-Litovsk.

A bitter armed struggle had by now begun between the new Soviet Government and the Whites, as their opponents were commonly called. The Bolsheviks or Reds, who, to deny their adversaries a rallying point, had in July murdered Tsar Nicholas and his family, were profoundly unpopular with large sections of the population, notably the peasants. Under General Denikin, the Whites, who found support in the Cossack country of the Kuban and the Don, soon began to gain strength. By October 1919, Denikin, advancing from the south, had reached Orel, barely two hundred miles from Moscow, which, after an interval of two hundred years, had once again been made the seat of government. Meanwhile, the Western Allies, disturbed by Lenin's separate peace, had despatched small expeditionary forces to a number of Russian ports still held by the Whites, in the pious hope of somehow getting rid of the Bolsheviks and bringing Russia back into the war.

For a while victory seemed within Denikin's grasp, but by this time the Red Army, as it was called, had, thanks largely to Trotski, now People's Commissar for War, grown to be a formidable fighting force, and in November 1919 the Red Cavalry achieved a decisive breakthrough. The following year Denikin, who had long since lost his earlier advantage, fell back on the Crimea, whence he in due course withdrew, with as many of his officers as could find their way there, to Constantinople. By the end of 1920, the Civil War was to all intents and purposes over, and the Bolsheviks were everywhere in more or less effective control of the country.

SOVIET UNION

The Bolshevik Revolution and its aftermath gave the subject races of the former Russian Empire new hope of winning their independence. Nationalist and separatist movements now emerged in most of the ethnically non-Russian regions. Transcaucasia, for one, had been thrown into utter confusion. Even before the Peace of Brest-Litovsk, the Russian armies fighting the Turks on the Caucasus front had started to desert and disintegrate, the demoralised troops for the most part simply heading for home. At the end of 1917, power passed *faute de mieux* into the hands of a Transcaucasian Commissariat, an amorphous body of moderate Social Democrats, composed in roughly equal proportions of Christian Georgians and Armenians and Moslem Azerbaijanis, all equally ill disposed to both the new Bolshevik Government in Petrograd and to the Whites who were fighting them, but with little else to keep them together.

The Great War still had at this time another twelve months to run. In April 1918, after some debate, the Transcaucasian Commissariat decided to cast loose from Russia and proclaim Transcaucasia an Independent Democratic Federative Republic. The months that followed were to offer all concerned plentiful scope for military and political intrigue and manoeuvre. From the first the new independent republic's prospects of survival were modest. Both Germans and Turks, not unnaturally, took every opportunity to further their own interest in what for them remained an important theatre of war. In May 1918, after much manipulation, the federation was dissolved and Georgia declared an independent state under German protection. Armenia and Azerbaijan likewise proclaimed themselves independent republics. Transcaucasia was in turmoil, Azerbaijan in particular. In July 1918 a group of local Bolsheviks, who had earlier established themselves in Baku, were chased out by a force of Turko-Tatar guerrillas with active Turkish support. After which, the city was taken over by an uneasy coalition of local social revolutionaries and Armenian nationalists, backed by a small British expeditionary force, who were then in their turn driven out by another force of Turks and Turko-Tatars.

With the Allied victory in November 1918, the situation underwent a further change. By the end of the year, all German and Turkish forces had been withdrawn from Transcaucasia. Baku and Georgia were then occupied by British troops, and a British High Commissioner was appointed for Georgia, Armenia and Azerbaijan. In the course of 1919 the British Government, having by now realised that there was little hope of overthrowing the Bolsheviks in Russia, came to regard the three Transcaucasian republics as a potential barrier against Bolshevik expansion in the Middle East.

The trouble was that, having once achieved their independence, the three nascent republics devoted much of their time and energy to fighting each other. Already in 1918 the Moslem Azerbaijanis, egged on by the Turks, had seized the opportunity to massacre large numbers of Christian Armenians. Before long, fighting broke out between Georgians and Armenians over areas claimed by both. The following year a strong delegation from each republic made a noisy appearance at the Paris Peace Conference, and in January 1920 the Allies granted all three *de facto* recognition, while doing little or nothing to help them maintain their independence, by this time seriously threatened by Bolshevik Russia.

The Russians had by now arrived at a new and rather different appreciation of the situation, and in the spring of 1920 a Special Committee was set up by Moscow for the express purpose of imposing Soviet rule on Transcaucasia. Results followed quickly. In April the independent Government of Azerbaijan was overthrown by the Red Army and replaced by a Bolshevik administration directly controlled by Moscow. A few days later a similar coup against Georgia was unsuccessful, whereupon the Russians, changing their tactics, offered the Georgians full recognition and a formal treaty of friendship, which was duly accepted. Next they turned their attention to Armenia, which by this time had been invaded by the armies of Kemal Ataturk. While the Armenians were vainly trying to come to terms with the Turks, the Red Army simply crossed the border in strength from Baku and declared Armenia, like Azerbaijan, a Soviet republic.

Of the three Transcaucasian republics, only Georgia, under British occupation, retained her independence. But in July 1920 the last British troops left. From the start, Kirov, the newly appointed Soviet ambassador in Tbilisi, made all the trouble he could for the Georgian Government. In this he was actively helped by the Georgian Communist Party and by northern Georgia's sizeable minority of racially distinct and essentially hostile Ossetians, stirred up by agitators from the Russian side of the border.

In January 1921 the Western Allies at long last made up their minds to grant Georgia *de jure* recognition. But it was by now too late. A couple of weeks later, in accordance with a carefully prepared plan, strong Soviet forces crossed the Georgian border at several points. Georgia's little army held out bravely for as long as it could against overwhelming odds. But on 24 February Tbilisi fell to the invaders, Georgia was proclaimed a Soviet republic, and on 17 March the remaining members of the former Georgian Government were evacuated from Batumi. Across the border in Armenia, these events sparked off a fresh rising against Soviet rule which it took the Red Army two months to extinguish. But by the spring of 1921, Armenia, Georgia and Azerbaijan had all three vanished into the maw of their northern neighbour.

Not unnaturally, the Georgians continued to resent Russian rule. Three years later, in the summer of 1924, there was a massive national uprising against government from Moscow. But after three weeks' fierce fighting, with heavy casualties on both sides, the insurrection was successfully crushed by the Red Army, and savage reprisals were inflicted on the survivors, leaving feelings of bitter resentment which the present writer found still alive a dozen years later.

Across the Caspian in Central Asia, as in Transcaucasia, the Revolution and Civil War, and the turmoil that followed them also offered the subject races an opportunity to assert their independence, of which they availed themselves to the full. Though a small British force based on Krasnovodsk still kept a hold on the Transcaspian Railway, Soviet rule had, after an initial period of uncertainty, been firmly established in Tashkent, since General von Kaufman's day the administrative centre of Russian Turkestan. Meanwhile, half a century after accepting Russian suzerainty, both the Emir of Bokhara and the Khan of Khiva had successfully reasserted their sovereignty. It was, however, to be of short duration. In the summer of 1920, after nearly three years of uneasy coexistence with his Bolshevik neighbours, the Emir of Bokhara was driven from his throne by the Red Army, later taking refuge in the mountains to the south, where for some years resistance was continued on his behalf by isolated bands of *Basmatchi* or bandits. The Khan of Khiva managed, for his part, to hold out until 1922, when he too was driven into exile, and his khanate transformed into the Soviet Republic of Khorezm. Like Bokhara, Khorezm was later to be absorbed into the larger Soviet

Republic of Uzbekistan, the British having long since withdrawn from Transcaspia.

Having defeated the Whites and their British, American and Japanese allies in Siberia, the Red Army managed in the long run to reoccupy what are now the republics of Kirghizia, Kazakhstan, Tadzhikistan and Turkmenistan, with the result that, within five years of the Revolution, the whole of what had once been known as Russia in Asia had successfully been brought under Soviet rule. After a period of troubled independence under the notorious Baron von Ungern-Sternberg, Outer Mongolia, formerly a Russian protectorate, became one once again, under the guise this time of the nominally independent People's Republic of Mongolia – famous for a score of years as the only other Communist-governed country in the world.

To the non-Russian races of the north and west, Finns, Estonians, Latvians and Lithuanians, the Bolshevik Revolution of 1917 brought, as it did to the Poles and Ukrainians, a very real hope of freedom from the incubus of Russian rule, under which most of them had lived willy-nilly for the best part of two centuries. During the last twelve months of war, following the disintegration of the Russian armies in 1917, most of the areas in question were overrun by the Germans, who not unnaturally took every opportunity to encourage nationalist and separatist tendencies wherever they found them.

Though the provisions of the Treaty of Brest-Litovsk and the various other dispositions made by the Germans did not survive their defeat, the Peace Conference, when convened, gave recognition, as far as was practicable, to the principle of national self-determination. In Russia's former Baltic provinces, three new independent republics now emerged: Latvia, Lithuania and Estonia. These were in due course recognised by the Allies and, indeed, by the Soviet Union itself. Finland, which had enjoyed some measure of autonomy under the tsars, now became fully independent. In the Ukraine, a national Ukrainian Government, set up under German auspices during the last months of the war, never received regular recognition from the Western Allies and was bloodily suppressed by the Bolsheviks in the course of the Civil War and its aftermath.

Well before the German defeat, the Western Allies had recognised Poland's undoubted right to nationhood, and in June 1919 an official Polish delegation signed the Treaty of Versailles on the country's behalf, even though its actual frontiers had not as yet been defined. The exact extent of Poland's national boundaries was to remain in doubt for some time, in particular the question of the Polish-Soviet frontier, which in the end led to actual war between the two countries, much of it fought on their traditional battleground, the Ukraine. Under the Soviet-Polish peace treaty of March 1921, the disputed territories of eastern Galicia and Volhynia were in the end given to Poland, while the bulk of the Ukraine became part of the Soviet Union.

STALIN AND HIS LEGACY

Six years of war, revolution and civil war had left Russia in a very bad way. The Bolsheviks' drastic and unpopular policy of War Communism had not produced the results hoped for. As an emergency measure, Lenin's New Economic Policy involved a limited and, it was emphasised, purely temporary return to capitalism. But for a time it gave the country the respite it needed. Meanwhile, the now all-powerful Communist Party, which was in a sense the cement which held the whole structure together, was by one means or another steadily extending its own authority, and with it that of the Soviet Government, to every corner of the country. Like Church and State under the tsars, Party and Government worked closely together under the new regime.

By 1924, conditions were sufficiently settled for the formation of a Union of Soviet Socialist Republics, which was in due course to receive official recognition from most of the great powers. It consisted of the original Russian Soviet Federated Socialist Republic (which included Siberia), the Ukraine, which, after a short spell of nominal independence under German sponsorship, had been reabsorbed, Belorussia (White Russia) and, following a brief period of independence, the new republics of Transcaucasia and Central Asia. Finland, Poland and the Baltic states, on the other hand, having won their independence, managed for the time being to keep it.

In January 1924, just as the final touches were being put to the world's first Communist state, which he had done so much to bring into being, Lenin, already a sick man, died at the early age of fifty-three. His death left a void, though not for long. To most people Lenin's obvious successor would have seemed to be Trotski, who had served under Lenin as People's Commissar both for War and for Foreign Affairs. But in Josip Vissarionovich Stalin, the wily, ruthless Georgian who since 1917 had held the office of Commissar for Nationalities, Trotski had a formidable rival. Just how formidable he did not perhaps realise until it was too late. For the past two years Stalin had been Secretary General of the Party, a position, as he had quickly grasped, of great potential power. By skilful use of it, he achieved within five years the result he was aiming at. 'Who, whom?' Lenin had asked. Once Stalin had gained control, there could no longer be any question as to what the answer would be. For the next quarter of a century Stalin was to wield total power, power greater and more absolute than any of his imperial predecessors, power that reached out into the ultimate recesses of the Union, power that was to grow with every year that went by. 'Imagine Jenghiz Khan with a telephone,' Tolstoi had said a score of years earlier with uncanny foresight.

It now became Stalin's purpose to transform an old-fashioned, mainly agricultural country into a modern, self-sufficient, industrial state, capable of holding its own in a hostile and highly competitive world. And to do this as fast as possible. Along with a series of five-year plans for industrialisation, he now relentlessly forced through, at high speed and at enormous cost in human lives, the collectivisation of Soviet agriculture, a project designed, amongst other things, to cure the Russian peasant of the bourgeois concept of private property, and at the same time to release more labour for industry. By 1933, collectivisation had, at enormous cost in human lives and suffering, become an accomplished fact. The First Five-Year Plan had been completed and the Second begun. In Germany, meanwhile, the advent of Adolf Hitler had greatly increased the likelihood of war. In the latest Soviet Five-Year Plan maximum emphasis was placed on defence.

By 1939, Stalin, the *Vozhd* or Leader, as he was commonly called, had held supreme power for ten years. But he was still taking no chances. Believing himself to be surrounded by enemies, saboteurs and spies, he had, from 1934 onwards, instituted throughout the Soviet Union a reign of terror unparalleled even in Russia's bloodstained history. Fear and suspicion possessed the whole country. Delation and denunciation were commonplace even among friends and relations. No one was safe; no one could trust anyone else; everyone, save only Stalin himself, waited for the dreaded knock at two o'clock in the morning. At a series of nightmarish state trials, the flower of Party, Government and the fighting services were dragged into court and made to confess to every conceivable crime, before being taken away and shot by the NKVD or People's Commissariat for Internal Affairs, as Stalin's ubiquitous and all-powerful secret police were now known.

The last thing Stalin wanted was war. By the Soviet-German Pact of August 1939, he had hoped to secure for himself half of Poland, Finland, the Baltic states and part of Rumania, and at the same time to keep Russia out of a conflict which, with any luck, would weaken both sides, greatly to Russia's advantage. In the event, however, his unholy alliance with Hitler made war a certainty for everyone.

On 22 June 1941 Hitler invaded Russia with 175 divisions. By September the Germans had reached the outskirts of Leningrad, and by October, of Moscow. For a couple of months the result hung in the balance. Then Soviet reinforcements reached the front from further east, and that winter, the worst in living memory, the German advance was held. Once the Soviet Union was involved, World War II, until then the Second Imperialist War, had become for its peoples the Great Patriotic War, engaging the country's entire resources, human and material. Leningrad remained beleaguered and further south the Red Army continued to withdraw until, late in the summer of 1942, a stand was made at Stalingrad on the Volga, the German advance halted and the threat to the Caucasus and its oil fields averted.

At Stalingrad, after a six months' siege, a German army of one hundred thousand men was encircled and in the end forced to surrender. It became a turning point in the war. By the early summer of 1944, the Germans had begun their withdrawal. In June a Second Front was opened in the West, and the Red Army began its advance through Eastern Europe. In the spring of 1945 the victorious armies of the Soviet Union and the Western Allies met on the Elbe, their meeting being quickly followed by Germany's unconditional surrender. In the Far East, the Soviet Union's neatly timed declaration of war on Japan, six days before the Japanese surrender, was to bring the Russians considerable territorial and other advantages.

The German withdrawal from Soviet soil enabled Stalin to resume possession of any Soviet territory that had in the course of the war fallen into enemy hands, and at the same time to make any further frontier adjustments he felt like. In 1941 the Germans had overrun the Baltic states, of which, after twenty years of independence, the Soviet Union had gained possession a year earlier under the terms of Stalin's secret deal with Hitler. In 1944 the victorious Red Army overran them in its turn and, though Great Britain and the United States refused to recognise their annexation, all three now once more became an integral part of the Soviet Union. The Finns, who, following their Winter War with the Soviet Union, had sided with the Axis, were allowed to survive as an independent country, though deprived of eastern Karelia and restricted in certain respects by the terms of the treaty they were now forced to conclude. Poland,

View of the Kremlin and the Great Stone Bridge, demolished in 1859. Moscow. Lithograph.

soon to be converted into a Soviet satellite, while gaining territorially at the expense of Germany, was likewise obliged to surrender considerable areas to the Soviet Union, including eastern Galicia and Volhynia, which now became part of the Soviet Ukraine. By thus annexing part of Poland, the Russians were, however, laying up trouble for themselves in the now extended Ukraine. The former Polish and Ukrainian population proved difficult to assimilate, and active resistance to Soviet rule continued for several years after 1945. Rumania was likewise relieved of Moldavia, which, with its mainly Rumanian population, was also sooner or later liable to become a cause of trouble.

The victories of the Red Army and the Russian people's heroic endurance had won the admiration of the West. But no sooner was the war with Germany over than a Cold War started between the former allies. In addition to Russia's substantial territorial gains, Stalin had also sought to protect himself against the supposed threat of capitalist encirclement by creating on his frontiers an extended empire of Communist satellite states, reaching from the Baltic to the Balkans. In Winston Churchill's words, an 'Iron Curtain' had come down across Europe.

Stalin's death in 1953 left as big a void as Lenin's had done thirty years earlier. The man who eventually filled it was of an entirely different character from his predecessor. Utterly ruthless and preternaturally suspicious, Stalin had believed in taking no risks. The new Secretary General of the Party, Nikita Sergeyevich Khrushchov, was by nature a gambler and an extrovert, a man prepared, in the ultimate analysis, to take a chance. In attempting, as he now did, even partially to liberalise a totalitarian dictatorship, he took an immense risk. At the same time he made it his business to improve, or at any rate to normalise, the Soviet Union's relations with the West. Peaceful co-existence, it was announced, had taken the place of Cold War.

For some ten years Khrushchov's bold experiment seemed to be paying off, both at home and abroad. But in the long run it endeared him neither to his own people nor to his immediate colleagues. In October 1964 a majority of the latter conspired to bring him down. Abruptly removed from office, he was replaced by the principal conspirator, Leonid Ilich Brezhnev.

In his eighteen years as Party leader and later as state president, Leonid Brezhnev was less successful in setting the clock back than he might have hoped. Despite an all-round tightening up, the evolutionary process which Khrushchov had initiated continued, though at a slower pace. On the whole, the standard of living improved, while the armed strength of the Soviet Union continued to increase. Brezhnev will be remembered, above all, for the so-called Brezhnev doctrine, under which the Soviet Union claimed the right to intervene, by armed force if necessary, in the affairs of any satellite country that showed signs of deviating from the straight and narrow path of orthodox Communism. This was first applied to Czechoslovakia in 1968, and more spectacularly, though a good deal less successfully, in Afghanistan eleven years later, when the Russians rashly involved themselves in an expensive and damaging war that was to drag on for a decade and do infinite harm to their image.

Following his death in 1982, Brezhnev was succeeded as Party Secretary and head of state by Yuri Vladimirovich Andropov, who for some fifteen years had presided over the KGB, as the notorious state security police had by now come to be known. Already old and sick, Andropov died within little more than a year of taking office, when his place was taken by the even older Konstantin Ustinovich Chernenko. Chernenko's death barely a year later, in March 1985, seemed to underline even more the geriatric character of the Soviet regime. In fact, it was to mark the end of one era and the beginning of a new one. Within hours of Chernenko's death, it was announced on behalf of the Central Committee that his place as Party Secretary had been taken by Mikhail Sergeyevich Gorbachov, then a vigorous, decisive, self-confident man of fifty-four.

INTO A NEW FUTURE

By the spring of 1991, Mikhail Sergeyevich Gorbachov, by then also President of the Soviet Union, had been Party Secretary for six full years. Whatever the ultimate outcome, a new era in Soviet, indeed world history, had begun, and the changes Gorbachov brought about in his first six years in power will without doubt cause him to rate in the judgement of history as one of the most significant political figures of the twentieth century.

That such changes should have come when they did and that he should have been their originator was, when you come to think of it, not altogether surprising. With Gorbachov, power in the Soviet Union passed to a new generation, differing profoundly from its predecessors in experience and outlook. A small child at the time of Stalin's horrendous purges, the new Party Secretary had reached maturity in Khrushchov's time, in a relatively relaxed atmosphere. Able and ambitious, the son and grandson of well-regarded members of the Communist Party, he had an excellent start in life, sharing with his intelligent and stylish wife Raisa the benefits of a university education. If there was ever to be a radical change in the nature of the Soviet regime (and the need for one was evident enough), the time for it was surely now.

The social, political, economic and, above all, psychological legacy which Gorbachov inherited when he came to power in 1985 was a daunting one. He had taken on, it is no exaggeration to say, just about the toughest job in the world. Despite limited successes achieved in different fields, the Soviet system, after seventy years spent 'Building Socialism', was simply not working. Though this was not yet generally recognised, Communism had conclusively been proved a failure. The question was how to put things right. It was not just a matter of new policies and new measures. What was needed in every republic of the Union was an entirely new approach, a new basic attitude and a new frame of mind.

Such was the background to Gorbachov's twin policies of *perestroika* and *glasnost* – of restructuring on the one hand, and of openness and frankness on the other – all, he was careful to add, for he was Secretary General of the Party, 'within a Socialist framework'. In his daring experiment (and you have to know Russia and the Russians to realise just how daring it was), the key question was bound to be: how far and how fast? For, as Alexis de Tocqueville had pointed out in a similar context a century and a half before, there is no trickier political operation than the liberalisation of an authoritarian regime. And here Gorbachov could not but recall the unhappy example of Khrushchov, who, after ten years spent pushing through badly needed reforms, had in the end been pulled down from within by his own closest associates. That was something which, as Gorbachov well knew, could easily happen to him too. As M. Jean-Paul Sartre had aptly put it, *'C'est la déStalinisation qui déStalinisera les déStalinisateurs.'*

From the outset, Gorbachov showed himself a shrewd enough political operator, quick to rid himself of awkward opponents, though almost as big a worry for him as any political opponent was the presence in the ranks of a grossly inflated bureaucracy of large numbers of people who, whether from inertia or self-interest, liked things the way they were and did not want them changed.

Inevitably, right from the start *glasnost* went much further and much faster than *perestroika*. With the best will in the world, it was bound to be a long time before the sluggish Soviet economy and no less sluggish Soviet system of government assumed the new look that Gorbachov was demanding of them. The new Party Secretary showed himself a realist. The myth that everything was perfect, had always been perfect and would soon be more perfect still, no longer held water. What Gorbachov was bravely trying to do was to rationalise Russia, to put an end to practices and attitudes which, since the time of the Tatars, had held it back under tsars and commissars alike, and which, in a fast-shrinking, fast-moving world, has isolated it from the main stream of human progress.

His external policy was equally innovative. His new approach

104. *Gelati Monastery, Georgia.*
A procession of the clergy and faithful
makes its way around the monastery on
a feast day. Within the monastery
precincts stand three churches and the
ruins of the famous academy founded in
the twelfth century by the philosopher
Joane Petritsi.

105. *Gelati Monastery, Georgia,*
a religious procession bearing crosses,
flags and flabella. Georgia embraced
Christianity around the year 330 and
still has its independent (autocephalous)
national Church, founded in 487, within
the Orthodox communion.
(pp. 154–155)

106. *His Holiness Ilya II, Patriarch of*
All Georgia. From the fourth century
on, Georgia was an important outpost of
Christianity in the Middle East. The
Church has played a central part in the
life of the people, their faith helping
them to preserve their national identity
through the centuries.(pp. 156–157)

and the revolutionary changes he had introduced in the Soviet Union were bound to have their effect on Stalin's extended empire of Soviet satellites, hitherto precariously kept in being by periodical recourse to the Brezhnev doctrine. By his decision to withdraw from Afghanistan in 1988, Gorbachov marked the end of the Brezhnev doctrine. Even so, many western observers found it hard to believe that the Kremlin would ever willingly relinquish control over such strategically vital satellites as East Germany or Poland. But in 1989 the destruction of the Berlin Wall and spontaneous reunification of Germany, Poland's rapid transition to democracy and to a market economy, and Moscow's acceptance of both made it clear that Brezhnev's doctrine was beyond doubt a thing of the past. Meanwhile, the other countries of the Eastern Bloc were fast following suit, each busy working out its own salvation after its own fashion. Soon the Warsaw Pact was formally dissolved, leaving its former adversary, NATO, to guarantee the security of Eastern no less than Western Europe. The Cold War, it could confidently be asserted, was at an end. A new world order was in the making.

From the first, Gorbachov's biggest single problem was how to get the Soviet economy moving. Abroad, he quickly made a name for himself. At home, however, after six years in power, he still had little to show for his pains. Food and consumer goods were in ever shorter supply and, thanks to *glasnost*, people were saying so at the top of their voices. It was a vicious circle, a chicken and egg situation. For the workers to produce more, Gorbachov needed to offer them more goods and services to spend their pay on. But, to offer them more goods and services, he needed more productive workers. Somehow the pump had to be primed. Meanwhile, the conduct of all too many Soviet workers remained as negative as ever. 'They pretend to pay us, and we pretend to work,' was still far too often their attitude.

Oddly enough, the full extent of the problems facing Gorbachov and the opposition he was encountering became evident only after he had been in power for nearly five years. It was in the winter of 1989/90 that it first began to look as though some of the forces he had released were beginning to get seriously out of hand, as though the latest developments were taking him by surprise, and he was being forced to improvise. Perhaps he had not fully realised the nature or extent of the task he had taken on, or foreseen the knock-on way in which one thing would lead to another, and every little painted Russian doll reveal, when opened, another ugly, grinning face inside.

Nor was his task made any easier by the chain reaction set off by his policies throughout Eastern Europe. Suddenly he found himself sailing on seas uncharted and unknown.

And here it is necessary to remember that for most Soviet citizens, more than seventy years after the Revolution, such concepts as a market economy, profit and loss, free competition, freedom of speech, political or economic pluralism, private enterprise, private property, even, were still by and large completely alien. Which made it impossible to foretell with any degree of accuracy how they might react to the various novel experiments, including, to some degree, the harsh medicine of the market, that were all at once being tried

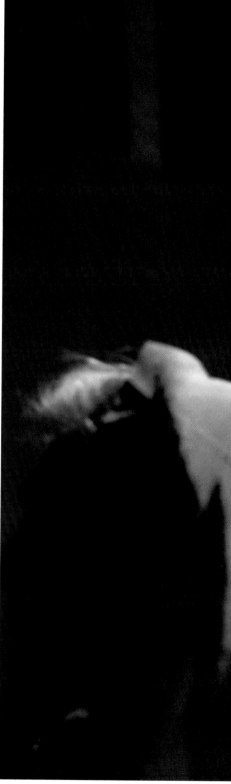

107, 108. *Church dignitaries
accompanying Patriarch Ilya II. Before
487, Georgia was a bishopric
subordinate to the Archbishop of
Antioch. Since the eleventh century, its
religious leader has been styled
Katholikos-Patriarch.*

109. Blessing the congregation in Gelati Monastery. Throughout Georgian history, the numerous monasteries remained strongholds of the Christian faith and centres of scholarship and art.

110. *Church service in Georgia. Despite seven decades of anti-religious education and propaganda, support for the Church, a symbol of the national being, has remained strong in Georgia.*

111. *Procession of the clergy and faithful setting out from the church of Gelati Monastery. Gelati was founded early in the twelfth century by one of Georgia's greatest kings, David IV, the Builder, who personally supervised its construction and was buried here in 1125.*

112. *Ushguli, Svanetia, a village 6,000 feet about sea level on the south-western slopes of the Greater Caucasus range. This region of Georgia, dotted with fortified dwellings and churches, was long an outpost of resistance to Turkish and Persian conquerors. Ushguli has seven small churches, some dating back to the tenth century.*

113. *Akhpat Monastery, Armenia, one of the loveliest architectural ensembles in this republic. Founded in the tenth century on a high rocky plateau, Akhpat resembles a small fortified town. The oldest and finest of its three main churches is the Cathedral of the Cross (977–991), built by King Smbat and King Gurgen, who are represented holding a model of it in a carving.*

114. The convivial and easy-going Georgians never miss an opportunity for celebrating with food and the excellent local wine, laid on here in a churchyard following a feast-day service.

115. A girl from Kutaisi. The Georgians are a remarkably good-looking race with an instinctive style and elegance. Generally tall and slim, with dark hair and fair skin, they are renowned as dancers and athletes, artists and musicians.

116. Procession around the main church of Gelati Monastery. Such processions, a regular feature of certain Orthodox feasts, are sometimes held in exceptional circumstances to invoke divine aid. This tradition dates back to the time of Byzantium, when the Patriarch, accompanied by clergy bearing the holiest ikons, would lead a procession around the walls of Constantinople when the city was threatened.

117. The Georgian National Dance
Company performs in front of the
famous eleventh-century cathedral
church of Alaverdi in the Georgian
province of Kakhetia. In every part of
Georgia there are age-old local traditions
of national dancing. Every village and
valley has its own variation of the reel,
round-dance or sword-dance.

118. Church of the Metekhi Virgin, Tbilisi, seen from the veranda of the Queen's Palace in the old quarter. This ancient church, rebuilt in its present form in the thirteenth century, stands within the Avlabar, the fifth-century citadel of Georgian kings, raised on a rocky bluff above the swift-flowing River Kura.

119, 120. A quiet day for traffic on the Georgian Military Highway, the great strategic road across the towering mountain barrier of the Caucasus which the Russians started building some two centuries ago. A remarkable feat of engineering, the highway, 120 miles in length, connects Ordzhonikidze (Vladikavkaz) with Tbilisi.

168

121. *In Svanetia, every village has its fortifications, testimony to centuries of struggle to maintain its independence. In times of trouble, many of Georgia's national treasures were carried off to this remote mountain region for safekeeping by the Svans, people of Georgian race who, because of their long isolation, speak an archaic form of the language.*

122. Painting by Niko Pirosmanashvili, the famous Georgian naïve artist. Pirosmani, as he is usually called, was born in 1862 in the village of Mirzaani, Kakhetia, but spent most of his life in Tbilisi, where he died of drink in 1918.

123. In the courtyard of the Convent of Samtavro, Mtzkhet (Mschet), the old capital of Georgia.

124. Portrait of J. V. Stalin beside the Ossetian Military Highway, which crosses the Caucasus. Like the Georgian Military Highway, it was constructed in the nineteenth century, at the time of the Russian conquest of the region.

125. Svanetia, Georgia, where every home was a castle, or at least had its own tower several stories high. (pp. 172–173)

"Сталин, для нас бы...
АВТОРИТЕ...
Г.К...

ХУД. Дзебисов

173

126. *Ananuri, Georgia, a citadel built in the sixteenth century. Within its walls rise a massive square watch-tower and two churches. Just behind the altar of the larger church there is a spy-hole so that even during services a look-out could watch for the approach of a foe.*

127. *Cathedral of Alaverdi, Kakhetia, built in the early eleventh century by King Bagrat III of Georgia in the shape of a gigantic cross.*

128. *Church of St George, Gelati Monastery. The high drum and conical 'dome' are characteristic of Georgian church architecture, remarkable for its complex ground-plans.*

129. *A Caucasian landscape. Stretching from the Black Sea to the Caspian, the Greater and Lesser Caucasus ranges divide Europe from Asia, Christendom from Islam. This is a land of legend: here Jason sought the Golden Fleece and Prometheus was chained by the gods to Mount Kazbek, the second highest peak.*

130. *The author's wife, Veronica, on one of their many journeys through the Soviet Union.*

131. *Georgian girls in a stylised version of the national costume. Stylisation seems somewhat superfluous, for the traditional Georgian attire is very elegant and perfectly suited to the proud bearing of this highland people.*

132. Ruins of an ancient fortress in the Northern Caucasus. The whole Caucasus is dotted with fortifications, many dating from pre-Christian times.

133. In the Northern Caucasus, a territory that includes the northern slopes of the Greater Caucasus range and, in the west, part of its southern slopes. In ancient times the Caucasus was regarded as the primaeval home of metallurgy. (pp. 178–179)

134. Mount Kazbek (Georgian: Mkinvari), rising to over 16,500 feet in the central part of the Greater Caucasus, is eternally snow-capped, with many glaciers descending its valleys. On its lower slopes, alpine pastures provide good grazing.

135. The Ossetian Military Highway, completed in 1897, winds its way through the Caucasus for 170 miles. Its highest point is the Mamison Pass, 9,250 feet above sea level.

136. A farm in the Caucasus. The raising of livestock, predominantly sheep, is the main occupation of the Georgian highlanders. Shepherds spend half their lives with their flocks on the high summer pastures. Whether thanks to the clean air, the altitude, or their diet of dairy produce, fruit and vegetables, a remarkable number live to be well over a hundred.

137. *A Caucasian village lying at over 6,000 feet. Nowhere else in Europe do people live so high in the mountains. As a result of physical isolation, numerous ancient peoples speaking a great variety of quite different tongues have survived in the Caucasus, called by the Arabs Jabal al Alsine: Mountain of Languages.*

out on them. It was, as Gorbachov's friend Alexander Yakovlev justly said, a leap into the unknown.

In the economic field, above all, enterprise, flexibility and initiative were after six years still badly lacking, as were the incentives and inducements normally offered under capitalism, not to mention the whole elaborate infrastructure of a capitalist economy. Only the black market delivered the goods. Which made it abundantly clear that *perestroika* 'in a socialist frame' would not be enough, and that sooner or later, but preferably sooner, it would be necessary for the Soviet Union, like its reborn East European neighbours, to jettison Marxism-Leninism and go over to a full-blown market economy and, in the long run, to political pluralism of one kind or another; that it would be necessary, in other words, to write off the existing political and economic system altogether. Clearly, this was bound to involve change on a mind-boggling scale and, if it was to succeed, massive cooperation from the capitalist world. There likewise remained the very real danger of an intermediate stage in which the old system would cease to function before the new had had time to get going.

Confronted with the imminent prospect of far-reaching changes in the Soviet Union, indeed with the unwelcome possibility of a second, and no less violent, Russian revolution, the Western powers decided, after due debate, to do what they could to rescue President Gorbachov from his predicament by helping to prop up his country's failing economy and smoothing, as best they could, the inevitably difficult transition from Communism to capitalism.

Gathering in London in July 1991, the Group of Seven leading industrial powers gave Gorbachov the opportunity he needed to inform them of his requirements, which in principle they accepted, without, however, going quite as far as he might have liked. There was, from the start, general recognition that what the Soviet economy needed most were not so much lavish credits as a massive injection of managerial and technological expertise. And this is what the West now undertook to provide. The West, declared President Bush, would 'try to help in every way we can'. 'The ice,' responded President Gorbachov, 'has started moving. The ice-breaker is underway.' Clearly, what would be required in the long run was large-scale foreign investment and the establishment of normal trade relations with the rest of the world. No less clearly, the Soviet Union would need to achieve a far greater measure of economic and financial stability before this became feasible. Meanwhile, the force of events had already carried the Soviet Union a considerable distance along the road to a kind of democracy. New political parties were fast emerging. Free elections were the order of the day, and a great debate was engaged on the shape of things to come.

Gorbachov's visit to London, which was followed by a successful visit by Bush to Moscow and a far-reaching agreement on strategic arms control, was without any doubt a turning point in history. Besides marking the end of the Cold War and of Communism as an economic and political system, it formally indicated the start of a new and positive relationship between East and West, and the admission,

138. Hagartsin Monastery, Armenia, founded in the eleventh century. Armenia was the first state to adopt Christianity as its official religion, in about the year 300. Its architects soon developed an original style of church building in the local black tufa, though there are few surviving examples that predate the seventh century.

185

in effect, of a transformed Soviet Union to the community of nations. 'Mikhail', President Bush called across to his Soviet opposite number, while Mikhail addressed the American President no less frequently as 'George'.

Back home, meanwhile, Mikhail, as unpopular as ever, was fighting desperately for his political life. In the Party, of which he remained Secretary General, there were among the hardliners those who openly disparaged what he had achieved, who angrily accused him of aping the West, while the radicals, for their part, still claimed that he was not moving fast enough in the desired direction.

For the Soviet Union, the passage from a one-party system to political pluralism was clearly liable to prove as painful as that from a command market to a market economy. Already the separation between Party and Government had become more marked, while the powers of Government and Parliament in relation to the Party had been correspondingly increased. To Gorbachov, as President, Parliament had, it is true, granted far-reaching powers, but these were in practice limited by the refusal of one republic after another to accept their validity.

If the situation was to be saved, speed was of the essence. Human beings are apt to feel strongly on two issues: first, their own standard of living and, secondly, their national identity, their right, as they see it, to a measure of self-determination. These are easily understood causes for which ordinary citizens will, when push comes to shove, take to the streets – something which in the Soviet Union had by this time become a perfectly practicable proposition.

Politics are essentially a matter of priorities. Gorbachov had two

absolute priorities: first, somehow to provide a better standard of living for the peoples of the Soviet Union and, secondly, to find a workable way of meeting the ever more urgent demands for a greater measure of home rule from the various republics, where, under the new dispensation, local leaders had found an easy way to popularity in public support for nationalism, and had long since forgotten the old Marxist-Leninist myth that under Communism national differences would quickly disappear. There was, moreover, a close link between the two issues. What many of the non-Russian republics most resented was being tied to economic failure and inefficiency at a time when their now fully independent neighbours across the border were already moving towards prosperity. Ethnic minorities are inevitably less likely to want to break away from a flourishing than from an impoverished Motherland.

As was perhaps only natural, what in the early days of the Soviet Union used to be called the Problem of the Nationalities (and was dealt with at the outset in his own rough-and-ready way by Stalin as the competent People's Commissar) first came to a head in the three Baltic republics. Reoccupied by Russia under Stalin's notorious deal with Hitler, and subsequently overrun, conquered and reconquered, first by the Germans and then by the Soviet armies, their inhabitants had without doubt a good reason to feel aggrieved. Though on and off a part of the Russian Empire since the eighteenth century or earlier, neither Latvians, Lithuanians nor Estonians ever learned to love the Russians. Having chosen independence in 1918 and made a reasonable success of it between the wars, they now could not wait to throw off yet again the burden of Russian rule. As the President of

View of the Spasski Tower and its surroundings, Moscow, 1813. Engraving.

187

Lithuania hastened to point out, they were 'not seeking to establish independence, but working to restore it'.

From Gorbachov's point of view, the problem posed by their pressing demands for independence were necessarily fraught with difficulty. In the long run, he was bound to have to grant all the republics of the Union a much greater measure of independence, possibly even something approaching Finlandisation. But in the early stages, the innumerable legal, fiscal, administrative, strategic and economic issues involved clearly called for a negotiated rather than a unilateral settlement.

There had long been active nationalist, indeed separatist movements in most of the non-Russian republics of the USSR, notably in the three Transcaucasian republics, which, like Poland, Finland and the Baltic republics, though in the long run less successfully, chose freedom in 1918. In April 1989 drastic repressive action imprudently taken by the Soviet army against peaceful demonstrators in Tbilisi had left Georgia seething with indignation, and free elections held eighteen months later brought an unequivocal demand for national independence. In Armenia and Azerbaijan, the problem had been further aggravated by the bitter mutual hostility of Armenians and Azerbaijanis, which at an early stage necessitated vigorous armed intervention by the Soviet military. In the Central Asian republics of Uzbekistan and Tadzhikistan, conquered by Russian arms in the nineteenth century and possessing a solidly Moslem population, the issue was, as in Azerbaijan, likely to be further complicated by the threat of Moslem fundamentalism, traditionally anathema to the Soviet state. There was likewise trouble in neighbouring Kazakhstan and Kirghizia. Nearer home, Moldavia, taken from Rumania under Stalin's deal with Hitler and retained by the Soviet Union after World War II, was bound to regard itself as Rumania *irredenta*. From Karelia, too, came corresponding demands for reunion with Finland. Most disturbing of all for Moscow, however, was the situation in the Ukraine, also once briefly independent. Without doubt, the inclusion in the Soviet Union after World War II of what had previously been part of the Polish Ukraine had further increased its instability and aggravated such nationalist tendencies as previously existed there. This became abundantly clear when the active resistance to Soviet rule manifested there during the war continued for several years after it was over. Linked with the resurgence of the long-banned Uniate Church, the existence of a strong Ukrainian separatist movement was an indisputable fact. But here the problem was on an altogether different scale. For the Soviet Union, the loss of the Ukraine with a Slav population of over 50 million, massive industrial development, some of the richest farmland in the country, the great harbour of Odessa and, finally, Kiev, the Mother of Russian Cities, would, as Lenin himself had pointed out back in 1918, represent a significant step towards disintegration.

Gorbachov, it is true, had put forward proposals for a new Union Treaty designed to transform the USSR into what he called a Union of Sovereign States, and even achieved a measure of consensus. But several republics quickly anticipated this move by declaring their independence unilaterally and insisting that their own constitutions took precedence over the Soviet Constitution, in other words, refusing to consider themselves bound by Soviet laws.

For a time, one of the strengths of Gorbachov's position had lain in the apparent absence of a credible alternative. But, following Boris Yeltsin's emergence as President of the Russian Federation at a time when ethnic Russian nationalism was stronger than ever, and his simultaneous resignation from the Party, this was manifestly no longer so. From the first, Yeltsin, who had clearly neither forgotten nor forgiven his elimination from the Politburo back in 1987 and whose popularity was greatly on the increase, showed himself more than ready to exploit Gorbachov's mounting difficulties by clamouring for more radical economic reforms and by negotiating directly with the Baltic republics and the Ukraine. By such means, and by raising the question of Russia's own national status within the Union, he deliberately threw the future of the Union open to debate. Russia, after all, contained over half the population of the Soviet Union and was materially richer than all the other republics put together. But such a debate could not in any case have been long delayed and, in a sense, proved salutary by serving as a catalyst and forcing all concerned to concentrate their minds urgently on this essential question.

On the pressing need for economic reform both Gorbachov and Yeltsin seemed to be roughly in agreement, though differing as to method and degree, and both had at one time or another declared their readiness to work together and give their combined support to a genuinely revolutionary programme of economic reform. In the ultimate analysis, both would obviously be judged by results, but these were yet to seek.

Which led to another aspect of the situation. If, as was conceivable, the Soviet Union (or what remained of it) were to go over to a genuine multi-party system, a logical consequence of this, however difficult to imagine, would be a more or less loyal opposition, indeed, an alternative government. Like so much else in the present fast-changing Soviet scene, this would to most Soviet citizens be a totally unfamiliar concept, though one to which, in time, they might need to get accustomed.

Whether, sooner or later, the time might not come for Gorbachov to distance himself from or even leave the increasingly unpopular and unrepresentative Communist Party, by now deprived of its constitutional monopoly of power, was already an open question. Of the profound significance of such a step by the Party's Secretary General and country's President there can be no doubt. But it was a step which his rival Yeltsin had already taken with evident success, while Gorbachov had for his part publicly declared his approval of his former Foreign Minister Shevardnadze's action in setting up a new and more democratically inclined party of his own. It would, moreover, be in a sense no more than a logical consequence of his policies hitherto.

Of considerable importance, obviously, at so critical a time was the attitude of the Soviet military. They were known to be unhappy about a lot of things – reforms, defence cuts, withdrawals and force reductions, all affecting their career prospects and way of life. Also the disagreeable police role forced on them in such places as the Baltic republics and Azerbaijan. But it was to be assumed that Gorbachov realised that a discontented army could be a dangerous thing, and had by this time made some sort of mutually satisfactory deal with Marshal Yazov, whom he himself had brought from relative obscurity to make Minister of Defence.

Such was the already precarious situation when, on the afternoon of Sunday, 18 August 1991, Mikhail Gorbachov, sitting quietly at the desk of his holiday home in the Crimea, composing, as it happened, a memorandum on the danger of a coup by Communist hardliners, answered a knock at the door, to be told that, on instructions from a self-styled Emergency Committee consisting of eight of his close government colleagues, he was under house arrest. The Junta, it appeared, was led by his Vice President, Genadi Yanayev, and included Marshal Dmitri Yazov, Minister of Defence, Vladimir Kryuchkov, Chairman of the KGB, Boris Pugo, Minister of the Interior, and Prime Minister Valentin Pavlov, all appointed to the posts they held by Gorbachov himself.

Strong units of the Soviet army with tanks and armoured personnel carriers now moved into key positions in Moscow; the members of the Junta established themselves in the Kremlin; it was announced that Gorbachov was sick and that Yanayev had become acting President; a state of emergency was declared, and all demonstrations were expressly forbidden.

On learning of what had occurred, different people reacted in different ways. The Communist Party and Government and numerous other leading Soviet personalities kept a low profile, showing by implication their approval of what had been done. Others waited to see what was going to happen next. Boris Yeltsin, on the other hand, having quickly secured the active support of the Russian (though not of the Soviet) Government and Parliament, lost no time in publicly condemning the coup and its perpetrators. Climbing onto the top of a tank outside the white marble Russian Parliament building, popularly known as the White House, he roundly denounced the conspirators as criminals, called for civil disobedience and a general strike, and demanded that President Gorbachov be immediately released and brought back to Moscow. After which, he went back inside to ring up the British Prime Minister and American President and ask for their support, which both gave unreservedly. 'There is not much time now,' he told John Major. 'The tanks will soon be here.' After this, events succeeded each other with startling rapidity. Soon, despite the ban on demonstrations, vast crowds of excited Muscovites, waving the old pre-revolutionary Russian flag, were spontaneously taking to the streets to protest against the Junta, build and man barricades, and yell for Yeltsin. It likewise soon became evident that the military were not of one mind. Some sought, rather halfheartedly, to carry out their instructions and others held back, while a number of the tank commanders outside the 'White House', instead of taking it by storm, actually turned their tanks round, facing outwards, so as to protect it as best they could against attack. By this time – it was Tuesday evening – night was falling and in the confusion a personnel carrier was set on fire by a well-aimed Molotov cocktail from the crowd; its commander panicked and gave the order to open fire, and three civilians were killed. This proved the turning point. From the first it had been clear that the troops were reluctant to fire on the crowd, and one commander after another now decided to pull out before things went any further. Soon the roads leading out of Moscow were full of armoured vehicles withdrawing as fast as they could, their crews waving in friendly fashion to the crowds lining the streets. What is more, those watching now noticed several sleek black Kremlin limousines threading their way as best they could through the retreating tanks. The chief conspirators were on their way out, defeated in the ultimate analysis by the Moscow crowd and by the army's refusal to obey orders.

It was now evident that the plot had failed – in Leningrad likewise, where Anatoli Sobchak, the city's radical mayor, had at once declared against the Junta. On Yeltsin's orders, an aircraft was despatched to the Crimea to bring back Gorbachov and, not long after that, Moscow television showed him arriving in Moscow, somewhat dishevelled but in good health physically and none the worse for his experience.

Of the Junta, Boris Pugo committed suicide, and the others were soon rounded up and placed under arrest to await trial on charges of high treason, while an extensive purge began of the Government, Army and security services. For good measure, the conspirators were now excommunicated by the Orthodox Patriarch, who, firmly aligning himself with the new regime, later presided over the state funeral of the three young men who had been killed during the coup. From start to finish, the whole astonishing interlude had lasted for little more than sixty hours.

As statues of Lenin were toppled everywhere and plans made to remove his body from its massive mausoleum on Red Square and let Leningrad revert to its old name of St Petersburg, it became clear that the events which had taken place during those sixty hours had been of enormous significance.

After seventy-four traumatic years, the Russians had finally

View of the Kremlin, Moscow. Engraving.

rejected Communism and all it stood for. After centuries of tyranny and oppression and only six years of a rather more enlightened regime, they had shown for all to see that they were not a race of serfs and were more than capable of taking their place in a free world. The Dictatorship of the Proletariat was at an end. That hackneyed phrase People Power had acquired a new meaning.

It remained to be seen what use would now be made of it. Also, how the ailing Soviet economy would fare under the new dispensation. (Had not the Junta gone out of their way to proclaim that they were acting to protect the living standards of ordinary people?) With Yeltsin now in the ascendant, there seemed every hope that the transition to a market economy would be accelerated, while the West, after a timely fright, would have the opportunity to show their relief at the turn events had taken and their good will to a new non-Communist regime by redoubling their efforts to help. Was it too much to hope that the Russians, having proved themselves democrats, might now show themselves entrepreneurs as well? For, even now, the danger of the whole country subsiding into anarchy and chaos remained a very real one.

Just what effect the coup and its failure would have on the narrower Soviet political scene was now a matter for intensive speculation at home and abroad. Clearly, Boris Yeltsin's personal standing had been enhanced by an impressive display of leadership, by his courageous and decisive conduct, and by his grasp of essentials at a moment of crisis. In a matter of hours he had emerged as a national hero and the saviour of his country. Although he had insisted that Gorbachov should be released from confinement and restored to his post, he had made it clear that this did not necessarily mean an end to their rivalry.

On the contrary, after Gorbachov had reaffirmed his loyalty to the Communist Party, Yeltsin promptly announced the Party's suspension in the Russian Republic, indicating that for him, Communism was a thing of the past in Russia and everywhere else. Taking full advantage of his much increased popularity, he also made it clear that, as the elected President of Russia, he now also intended to play a leading part in Union affairs. Not until forty-eight hours later did Gorbachov, having had time to make a more realistic assessment of the situation, move in his turn to abolish the Party, thus carrying through to its logical conclusion the revolutionary process which he had set in motion six years earlier, and at the same time depriving the Union, at one stroke, of the cement which had for so long held it together. 'In the past,' was Yeltsin's crisp comment, 'he did not understand the need for radical reforms. Now he does.'

It was difficult to tell what measure of cooperation would in the long run prove practicable between Gorbachov and Yeltsin. While Yeltsin's position had been strengthened by what had happened, Gorbachov's had without doubt been diminished. Nor, having rescued him, did Yeltsin miss many opportunities of scoring off his rival, to the extent even of blaming him for the coup of which he was so nearly the victim. Indeed, as events proved, Gorbachov in the end became a casualty of the revolution he originated. As he himself

141. *Cathedral of the Assumption,*
Vladimir, dating in its present form from
the fifteenth–sixteenth century. In the
mid-twelfth century, Prince Andrei of
Bogolyubovo, the most powerful
Russian prince of his time, moved his
capital to Vladimir and set about
strengthening its Kremlin and building
churches to rival those in the former
capital, Kiev.

142. *Church of the Resurrection, Rostov*
Veliki, c. 1670. Rostov, the only Russian
city besides Novgorod to bear the epithet
'the Great', is also one of the most
ancient, first mentioned in chronicles in
862. Rostov is famed for its bell-towers
and tradition of bell-ringing.

143. *Service in the Cathedral of the Trinity, Pskov. The original church on this site was completely rebuilt in the late seventeenth century.*

144. *Monastery of the Trinity and St Sergei, Zagorsk, until recently the seat of the Russian Patriarch. Early in the fifteenth century the newly-built Cathedral of the Holy Trinity was decorated by the most celebrated of Russia's early painters, Andrei Rublov, whose most famous ikon, The Old Testament Trinity, was kept here until taken to Moscow in 1929.*

145. *Old and new: Kalinin Prospekt, Moscow. Spared by the planners, a tiny onion-domed church, converted into an aquarium, nestles at the foot of one of the tallest skyscrapers.*

146. *The Golden Gate, Vladimir, built by Prince Andrei of Bogolyubovo in 1164 as part of the city's defences. This example of early military architecture is unique in Russia and has no direct analogue elsewhere in Europe. It served also as the ceremonial entrance to the city. Surmounting it is the little Gate-Church of the Rizopolozheniye.*

147. *Pskov Kremlin with the Cathedral of the Trinity. The earlier wooden fortifications of this citadel were replaced by stone ramparts in the fourteenth century and further extended in the fifteenth when Pskov was encircled by walls over five miles long with 39 towers. This 'younger brother' of nearby Novgorod served as a stronghold on the then north-west border of Russia.*

202

148. *Cathedral of St Dmitri, Vladimir, twelfth century. Built of white limestone by Russian masons in the reign of Prince Vsevolod, whose chapel royal it became, this is a superb example of the Suzdal-Vladimir style of architecture that was influential throughout Kievan Rus. Its façade is lavishly decorated with low-relief carvings of saints, prophets and a number of historical and legendary figures.*

149. *Church of St Nicholas, Pskov. In the period of the town's political independence (1348–1510), many churches were built, most of them quite modest buildings, in keeping with the democratic nature of the city's government.*

150. *Cathedral of the Assumption, Moscow Kremlin, frescoes above the main entrance. These and the paintings above the other portals were added to this magnificent church in the seventeenth century.*

151. *Cathedral of the Assumption, Zagorsk, completed in 1564. Similar in style to the Uspenski Sobor in Moscow, though somewhat larger, it is the burial place of Boris Godunov and his family.* (p. 204)

152. *Cathedral of the Assumption (Uspenski Sobor), the oldest cathedral of the Moscow Kremlin. It was built in 1475–79 by the Italian architect Fioravante on the site of an older church of the same name. From the sixteenth century it was the place where tsars were crowned.* (p. 205)

153. *A seventh-century Armenian church. The Armenians became highly accomplished builders of stone churches at a very early date: the sixth–seventh century is considered the classical age of a style of church architecture which did not diverge into distinct Armenian and Georgian styles until the tenth century.*

154. *Ananuri, Georgia. This citadel in eastern Georgia dates from the sixteenth–seventeenth century, when Iran exerted a strong political influence on this region. Certain new decorative elements of Iranian origin appear in its architecture. Besides military and residential buildings, the walls of Ananuri enclose two churches, one of considerable size.*

remarked, the country he returned to from the Crimea was a different one and, he added, he was a different man.

As to the future of the former Soviet Union, it is significant that the Junta's attempted coup was carefully timed so as to anticipate the signing of the proposed new Treaty of Union. Given Yeltsin's more positive attitude to the republics' demands for independence, it seemed clear enough that, while the Junta would have made some effort to re-establish Moscow's domination over them, any future Government would be far readier to give the republics what they wanted. Encouraged by the failure of the coup, successive republics now quickly asserted or reasserted their claims to independence, including, this time, the Ukraine. To this a much chastened Gorbachov, bowing once more to the inevitable, responded by promising them what they asked for, preferably, he insisted, within a re-negotiated Union.

Clearly, the last hope of holding together some part of the Soviet Union now lay in a version of what Gorbachov himself had called a Union of Sovereign States. Even if some of the republics were not to accede to such a union, it seemed probable that, having once asserted their independence, they would judge it in their interest to enter into mutual agreements with each other, thus constituting a loose confederation or commonwealth, which, after a fashion, would fill the place formerly occupied by the empire of the tsars and, for the last seventy years or more, by Lenin's ill-fated Union of Soviet Socialist Republics.

And this, in the event, is what happened. On 5 September 1991, Gorbachov and Yeltsin having jointly declared their determination to work together, the Congress of People's Deputies passed, as a first step, a law designed to transfer a far greater measure of power from the centre to the republics, and so leave the way open for a newly negotiated Treaty of Union. Meanwhile, as an interim measure, the existing machinery of government was swept away and replaced by a smaller two-chamber Parliament made up of deputies elected in the republics, an inter-republican economic committee, and a Council of State or collective presidency, still presided over by Gorbachov, though with reduced powers, and consisting of the political leaders of whichever republics eventually joined the Union.

Next day, the new Council of State formally granted independence to the three Baltic republics, whose leaders let it be known that they would in due course give consideration to the possibility of establishing some economic or other link with the Union. Where the Baltic republics had shown the way, others followed fast. And not only republics. To Moscow came demands for independence from the Volga Tatars, while in newly independent Georgia, the Southern Ossetians were likewise clamouring to be given their freedom. In a matter of hours, it could truly be said that the Union of Soviet Socialist Republics had ceased to exist. At the end of 1991, Gorbachov, his position no longer tenable, had no choice but to resign, leaving President Yeltsin of Russia as the dominant figure in the newly formed Commonwealth of Independent States.

155. Cathedral of the Nativity of the Virgin, Suzdal, built in the thirteenth century on the site of an even older church. Originally this was a three-domed structure that was so much admired it was taken as the model for cathedrals in Moscow, Yaroslavl and other cities. When its roof collapsed (1445), it was reconstructed with five domes, similar to Moscow churches.

APPENDIX

THE FORMER UNION OF SOVIET SOCIALIST REPUBLICS (USSR) as on 19 August 1991

Area: 8.6 million sq.mi.
Population: 268.8 million (1982)
Capital: Moscow (Moskva), *pop.* 8.3 million
Nationalities: Russians 52%, Ukrainians 18.5%, Uzbeks 5.5%, Belorussians 3.6%, Kazakhs 2.7%, all others less than 2%
Religions: Orthodox, Moslem, Catholic, Protestant, Buddhist, Jewish

REPUBLICS

The 15 republics of the USSR: the Russian Soviet Federated Socialist Republic (SFSR), and 14 Soviet Socialist Republics (SSR). Within these there are 20 Autonomous Socialist Soviet Republics (ASSR), 8 Autonomous Provinces (*Oblasts,* AO), and 10 National Districts (*Okrugs,* NO). In order of population size:

Russian SFSR (including 16 ASSRS, 5 AOs, 10 NOs)
Ukrainian SSR
Uzbek SSR (including 1 ASSR, I AO)
Belorussian SSR
Kazakh SSR
Azerbaijanian SSR (including 1 ASSR, 1 AO)
Georgian SSR (including 2 ASSRs, 1 AO)
Tadzhik SSR (including 1 AO)
Moldavian SSR
Kirghiz SSR
Lithuanian SSR
Armenian SSR
Turkmen SSR
Latvian SSR
Estonian SSR

ETHNO-LINGUISTIC GROUPS

The population of the Union is of great diversity. The Soviet Academy of Sciences recorded 169 ethnic groups. The Appendix provides statistical and other information on the 22 nationalities and minorities that number one million or more, given in alphabetical order. They may be classified as follows:

1. Indo-European family
   Slavic group: Russians, Ukrainians, Belorussians, Poles
   Armenian group: Armenians
   Baltic group: Lithuanians, Latvians (Letts)
   Germanic group: Germans
   Iranian group: Tadzhiks
   Latin/Romance group: Moldavians
2. Altaic family
   Tatar-Turkic group: Azeri, Bashkirs, Chuvash, Kazakhs, Kirghiz, Tatars, Turkmen, Uzbeks
3. Ural family
   Ugro-Finnish group: Estonians, Mordvins
4. Paleocaucasian family
   Kartvelian group: Georgians
5. Jews

ARMENIANS

The Armenians are descended from a people of Indo-European origin and the inhabitants of the ancient kingdom of Urartu, whom they assimilated after settling on its territory (7th c. BC). They call themselves Hay and their country Hayastan. To the ancient Persians and Greeks they were known as Armina/Armenioi. In the USSR they number 4.85 million (1985), the majority living in the Armenian SSR; there are also compact enclaves in Azerbaijan, Georgia and the North Caucasus. Two thirds of the Armenian population (est. 1,750,000) in the Ottoman Empire had been deported or massacred by 1916. The Armenian diaspora extends to some 70 countries (USA 650,000, France 250,000, Lebanon 120,000, etc.). The Armenian language, an independent member of the Indo-European family, has many borrowings from Iranian and numerous words of unknown origin. Its distinctive alphabet, still used, was invented in the early 5th c. The Armenians are Monophysite Christians and belong to the Armenian Apostolic (Orthodox) Church.

The Armenian SSR. Area: 11,506 sq. mi. Capital: Yerevan (Erivan). Population (1982): 3,169,000 (c. 80% Armenian, the rest mostly Russians, Azeri, Kurds). Half the country is over 6,000 ft a.s.l. (the Lesser Caucasus and Armenian Highlands), only 3% under 2,000 ft. The climate is continental, with a considerable diurnal range. Major rivers are the Araks, forming the border with Turkey, and its tributary the Razdan, which flows out of Lake Sevan (6,279 ft a.s.l.) and is exploited for hydro-electric power production. Agriculture is limited by the rugged terrain and scant rainfall in lowland areas. Wheat, maize and sugar beet are the main crops. On irrigated areas, cotton, tobacco, vines and mulberry trees are grown. Deposits of copper, lead, zinc and chrome are exploited and processed. The Transcauscasian Railway is the main surface communications line.

The historical borders of Armenia encompass Soviet Armenia and north-eastern Turkey, where the Armenian people settled in the 7th c. BC. They acknowledged the rule of Persia in the 6th c. BC and later that of Alexander the Great and the Seleucids. A united independent kingdom was established by Tigranes II the Great (reigned c. 94–56 BC). About 300 AD Tigranes III was converted to Christianity, which became the state religion. In the 7th c. the Arabs established their suzerainty. The period of the Bagratid kings (9th–10th c.), with their capital at Ani, was the golden age of Armenian history. The Seljuk Turks invaded in the 11th c., and the Mongols in the 13th. After the fall of Greater Armenia, the kingdom of Little (Lesser) Armenia was established (12th–14th c.), with strong Frankish-Crusader ties. In the following centuries Persia and the Ottoman Empire struggled for control of the territory, with Turkey the more successful. In 1828 Persia ceded the Yerevan and Nakhichevan khanates to Russia, which in 1878 acquired more Armenian-populated areas after the Russo-Turkish War. In 1895–96 and 1915–16 over a million Armenians in the Turkish Empire were massacred or deported. The independent Armenian republic proclaimed in 1918 was attacked by Turkey and Russia. Its territory was divided along the present border and the Armenian SSR was established in 1920. In 1922 it became part of the Transcaucasian SFSR, which joined the USSR later that year, and in 1936 became a constituent republic again. The Azeri-populated enclave of Nakhichevan was assigned to the Azerbaijanian SSR, from which it is physically separated.

Traditionally farmers and herders, the Armenians are also well known for their mercantile skill. The antiquity and brilliance of their cultural achievements are exemplified by the capital, Yerevan, founded over 2,770 years ago, and the many ancient churches displaying great architectural and sculptural skill and originality. Armenia was the the first country in the world to adopt Christianity as its state religion, following the conversion of its king by St Gregory the Illuminator. The seat of the Supreme Katholikos of the Armenian Church is at Echmiadzin, where one of the world's greatest libraries of illuminated manuscripts, the Matendaran, was assembled (now in Yerevan). The art of MS illumination reached its zenith in the 13th c., but fine examples can be found from the 9th to 17th c.

Armenian literature began to flourish soon after the creation of the Armenian alphabet by St Mesrop *c.* 410. The 5th c. was a great age of translation, but also the writing of original Christian works and history: the best-known secular work is the *History of Armenia* by Moses of Khoren. The outstanding example of folk poetry is the epic *David of Sasun,* ascribed to the 8th to 10th c. but not written down until 1873, recounting the wars against the Arabs. The first Armenian book was printed in Venice in 1512, and the first newspaper in India in 1794. In the 19th c., the use of the classical language in literature gave way to the spoken language (two main dialects). A pioneer in this in Russian Armenia was the novelist Khachatur Abovian.

AZERI (AZERBAIJANIANS)

The Azeri (Azerbaijanians or Azerbaijani Turks), together with the Armenians and Georgians the most numerous of the Caucasus peoples, inhabit the southern part of Transcaucasia. In the USSR they number 6.27 million (1985), the majority living in the Azerbaijanian SSR, with smaller numbers in the Armenian and Georgian SSRs. Over 8 milion live in the adjoining Iranian province of Azerbaijan. They belong to the western group of Turkic peoples and are of the Islamic faith (mostly Shi'ite). Their language, Azeri, is one of the Oghuz group of Turkic languages.

The Azerbaijanian SSR. Area: 33,436 sq.mi. Capital: Baku. Population (1982): 6.3 million (about 70% Azeri, the rest mostly Russians and

The Krasnaya Gate, built in 1709 to mark the victory at Poltava, demolished in 1934, Moscow. Lithograph.

212

Armenians). The republic includes the Nakhichevan ASSR (pop. 252,000, 90% Azeri) and the Nagorno-Karabak AO (pop. 165,000, 85% Armenians). Apart from the Kura lowlands in the south, Soviet Azerbaijan is mostly mountainous. Because of the great range of altitude, its climate and vegetation are extremely varied. The principal rivers are the Kura and Araks (Araxes). Besides oil, the main basis of its industrial development, there are significant deposits of iron, copper, lead and other ores, and of natural gas. The Baku oil field, formerly the chief source of Soviet oil (68% in 1940), now produces less than 15%. A double pipeline connects Baku with Batumi on the Black Sea. Crops include cotton, rice, tea, citrus fruit, tobacco and vines. Sheep and cattle raising, and fishing (on the Caspian Sea) are important.

Ruled in early times by the Medes, Persians, Macedonians and Parthians, in the 7th c. Azerbaijan was conquered by the Arabs, in the 11th by the Seljuk Turks, and in the 13th by the Mongols. From the 15th to 18th c. Persia and Turkey warred intermittently over the territory. After long wars of aggression, Russia acquired part of it by treaty in 1813. By the treaty of 1828, Azerbaijan was divided between Russia and Persia along the present border. After a brief period as an independent republic (1918–20), the Azerbaijanian SSR was established in April 1920. It formed part of the Transcaucasian SFSR with Georgia and Armenia from 1922 to 1936, when the Azerbaijanian SSR again became a separate federal unit.

The Azeri, producers of cotton, silk and wool, have a long tradition in the weaving of fine cloth and rugs. Other crafts include the making of gold jewelry and pottery. Like the inhabitants of neighbouring Daghestan and other parts of the Caucasus, they are renowned for their longevity. (Shirali Muslimov, who died in 1975 at the age of 168, is claimed to be the longest-lived person in recorded history.) Most of the oldest Azeri are highland pastoral folk, living on a diet of dairy produce, fruit and vegetables, with little meat. Few of them smoke or drink coffee or tea, though most drink wine in moderation all their lives.

Azerbaijanian (Azeri) literature in written form developed only in the 16th c. The Azeri poet Fuzuli (d. 1556) is one of the outstanding figures of Ottoman Turkish literature. Feth-Ali Ahundov (mid-19th c.) is a notable writer of comedies.

BASHKIRS

The Bashkirs, like their western neighbours the Tatars, are classified in the north-west group of Turkic people, though there are several anthropological types. In the USSR they number 1.47 million (1985), of whom 936,000 live in the Bashkir ASSR in the Russian SFSR, the others mostly in surrounding Russian *oblasts:* Chelyabinsk, Kurgan, Orenburg, Perm and Sverdlovsk. Their language, which had no written form until after the Revolution, belongs to the north-west (Kipchak) group of the Turkic family. They are of the Islamic (Sunnite) faith.

The Bashkir ASSR (Bashkiria). Area: 55,444 sq.mi. Capital: Ufa. Population (1982): 3,856,000 (38% Bashkirs, also Russians, Tatars, Chuvash). The Southern Urals in the east of the republic descend westward to the valleys of the two biggest rivers, the Belaya (882 mi. in length) and its chief tributary, the Ufa. The climate is extreme. The Belaya valley and the Belebei uplands in the west are the most fertile areas. Crops include cereals, sugar beet and sunflower. The republic is exceptionally rich in natural resources: the biggest oil deposits in the Urals (production outstripped Baku in 1955), accompanied by natural gas, also timber, coal, salt and numerous ores. Iron and copper mining began in the 18th c. The major industries are oil refining, chemicals, engineering, timber working. Ufa, the largest city and chief industrial centre, lies on a major trans-Ural railway and at the confluence of the navigable Belaya and Ufa rivers.

Formerly pastoral nomads, the Bashkirs are first mentioned in 10th-c. Arabic sources. They are believed to have moved into their present territory when it was ruled by the khans of the Golden Horde (13th–15th c.), but mostly retained their nomadic way of life until the 19th c. Russia took control of the region after 1552, when Ivan the Terrible destroyed the Kazan khanate and began colonisation, founding Ufa in 1574. Numerous Bashkir uprisings were ruthlessly quelled. Bashkiria became an autonomous Soviet republic (one of the first) in 1919.

In the past the Bashkirs had a strong clan and tribal social structure, which has now disappeared. They raised large herds of the small, strong Bashkirian breed of horse, and made *kumys* from fermented mare's milk. There is also a tradition of bee-keeping.

Having no writing, they developed a rich oral literature, especially heroic epics *(kubairi),* passed down by folk singers or bards *(seseni).* Notable figures in post-revolutionary literature include the poets G. Gumer, B. Ishemgulov, R. Nigmati, and the prose-writers I. Nasyri and S. Agish.

BELORUSSIANS

The Belorussians (Byelorussians, White Russians) are numerically the smallest of the East Slav peoples. In the USSR they numer 9.76 million (1982), of whom 7,568,000 live in the Belorussian SSR (1989). There are sizeable communities in Poland, the USA, Canada, Argentina and other countries. Poverty drove almost 1.5 million to move to the USA or Siberia in the half century before the Revolution. The Belorussian language, like Russian and Ukrainian, belongs to the eastern group of Slavic languages. Most are Orthodox, a minority Catholic.

The Belorussian SSR. Area: 80,154 sq. mi. Capital: Minsk. Population (1982): 9,744,000 (73% Belorussians, others mainly Russians, Poles, Ukrainians and Jews). Bounded by the Baltic states to the north, Poland to the west, the Russian SFSR to the east and the Ukraine to the south, Belorussia, part of the great East European plain, is intersected by numerous rivers and has over 4,000 lakes. There are extensive marshes, especially in the Polesye region in the south (Pripet marshes), and forests (one third of the territory). Drainage of marshes has increased the amount of fertile land. The chief crops are cereals, potatoes, flax, hemp and sugar beet. Livestock farming (cattle, pigs) is important. Timber and peat are the main natural resources. Industries include textile and footwear manufacturing, timber and food processing, engineering (farm machinery, trucks), chemicals. Minsk, Gomel, Vitebsk and Mogilev are the major industrial centres.

Belorussia was one of the first regions settled by the Slavs, who formed small principalities here in the 8th–9th c. From the 9th to 13th c.

214

they were vassals of Kievan Rus, until its overthrow by the Tatars (1240). Lithuania then gained control, and after 1386 it was part of the Polish-Lithuanian kingdom. In the latter half of the 18th c. Russia acquired the whole of Belorussia in the three successive partitions of Poland. The Soviets seized power in Minsk in 1917, and after the defeat of counter-revolutionary and German forces, the Belorussian SSR was proclaimed in 1919. Part of the territory was returned to Poland by the Treaty of Brest (1919) but by the Polish-Soviet treaty of 1945, the USSR regained all Belorussia except the Bialystok region. The Polish population mostly moved to Poland. In both world wars, Belorussia was the scene of heavy fighting, suffering enormous devastation and loss of life. Some 2.2 million of the population died in World War II, when there was a strong partisan movement in the republic.

The Belorussians have traditionally been peasant farmers: the rural population still forms a much higher proportion than in the USSR as a whole. Poverty led many to immigrate after the abolition of serfdom in 1861. Traditional crafts (woodcarving, carpentry, weaving, pottery, blacksmithing, etc.) have survived, and the colourful national costume is still worn on festive occasions and when performing the lively folk dances *(karagod, tanok)*. A type of puppet theatre *(batleyka)* is a popular form of entertainment.

The earliest Belorussian writing is from the 11th–12th c. Georgi (Francisk) Skorina made a translation of the Bible printed in Prague in 1517 (the third oldest printed Bible translation, after the German and Czech). As a result of Polish, then Russian, political and social repression, Belorussian literature did not begin to flourish until the mid-19th c. (V. I. Dunyin-Martsinkevich, Jan Barshchevski, A. Ripinski, Jan Chatot and, most notably, the poet Francisk Bugushevich). A new generation of writers, influenced by the events shaking the Empire, emerged in the early 20th c. The most eminent are Janko Kupal, Jakub Kolas and Maxim Bogdanovich.

St Petersburg seen from the River Fontanka. Engraving.

215

CHUVASH

The Chuvash are a Turkic people related to a branch of the Bulgars. In the USSR they number 1.79 million (1985), of whom 887,700 live in the Chuvash ASSR within the Russian SFSR, and smaller groups in the Saratov, Kemeron, Sverdlovsk and Tyumen *oblasts*. Their language is a relatively independent member of the west-Turkic group. Formerly Moslems, they were converted to Orthodox Christianity in the mid-18th c.

The Chuvash ASSR. Area: 7,066 sq. mi. Capital: Cheboksary. Population (1982): 1,315,000 (67% Chuvash, also Russians, Mari, Tatars, Mordvins). The autonomous republic occupies the area lying south of the middle Volga, between Gorki and Kazan, mostly low hills and plains, drained by Volga tributaries (Sura, Kubnya, Siyaga). The climate is moderate continental. Natural resources include timber, oil-shale and peat. Almost half the territory is arable land, and two thirds of the population engage in farming (grain crops, vegetables, hemp, livestock, poultry). Textiles, timber working, food processing and engineering are the chief industrial branches. The Volga and Sura are navigable, with Cheboksary and Alatyr the main river ports. The Moscow-Kazan-Trans-Siberian railway crosses the region.

The Chuvash are descended from tribes of the Turkic family (predominantly Bulgars) who moved into the area in the 5th c. These were related to the Bulgars who settled in the Balkans in the 6th–7th c. The country known as Bulgaria on the Volga was significant from the early 10th to the early 13th c. The Chuvash people further consolidated as a nation within the khanates of the Golden Horde and Kazan (13th–16th c.). In the reign of Ivan the Terrible they were incorporated in the Russian Empire (1551). After the Revolution they were given autonomous status (from 1920 – AO, from 1925 – ASSR).

The upland and lowland Chuvash differ somewhat in language and customs. Family life still preserves some patriarchal features. When the area came under Russia they were already a sedentary farming people, living in villages and hamlets *(yal)*. Their traditions include woodcarving and bee-keeping. A noteworthy form of their oral literature is 'calendar' poetry. Since the Revolution, written literature and intellectual life have developed.

ESTONIANS

The Estonians belong to the Ugro-Finnish (Finno-Ugric) family of peoples. In the USSR they number 1,030,000 (1985), of whom 947,800 live in the Estonian SSR. There are some 700,000 in other countries (USA, Canada, Sweden, Australia). Their language is closest to Finnish. Most are Protestants (Lutherans).

The Estonian SSR. Area: 17,413 sq. mi. Capital: Tallinn. Population (1982): 1,496,000 (68% Estonians, the others mostly Russians, Belorussians and Ukrainians). The smallest of the Baltic republics, it occupies a peninsula on the southern shore of the Baltic Sea, between the gulfs of Riga and Finland. The northern area is mostly marshy lowland, while the south has hills rising to *c.* 1,000 ft. The largest islands are Saaremaa and Hiiuma. There are over 200 lakes, of which Chudskoye (Peipsi jarv), connected by the Narva with the Baltic, is much the biggest. The climate is relatively mild for this latitude. Natural resources include oil-shale, timber and peat. Less than 20% of the land is cultivated (grain crops, fodder, potatoes), and livestock is more important than arable farming. Industry (engineering, textiles, shipbuilding) has grown considerably since 1945. Tallinn and Parnu are the chief ports.

The Estonians moved from the Volga region to the Baltic shores around the beginning of the 1st c. AD. Their territory was invaded by the Vikings (9th c.), and conquered by the Germans and Danes in the early 13th c. Most of the country then came under the rule of the Teutonic Knights, who reduced the local population to serfdom. In the early 16th c. Sweden gained control. Following the defeat of Charles XII by Peter the Great at Poltava (1709), Sweden formally ceded it to Russia in 1721. In 1917 Russia granted Estonia autonomy, but the following year it was occupied by Germany. From 1920 to 1940 Estonia was an independent republic. By secret terms of the German-Soviet non-aggression treaty of 1939, Finland, Estonia and Latvia were assigned to the USSR, whose forces occupied Estonia the following June. One year later Germany invaded the country and occupied it until the autumn of 1944, when Soviet forces regained the territory.

The Estonians have a relatively high standard of living in the USSR, due primarily to their manufacturing industry. They have close linguistic and cultural ties with the Finns. The traditional culture of the islands and western parts shows Scandinavian influence, while that of the southern and eastern regions has East Slavonic features. In the period of national awakening (19th c.), the rich oral literature was collected and written down. From narrative folk songs, F. R. Kreutzwald compiled a national epic, the *Kalevipoeg* (1857–61). Choral and folk music groups flourished from the mid-19th c. (the national song festival was first held in Tartu in 1869). Education made rapid progress in the latter 19th c., and illiteracy was almost eliminated. The first Estonian newspaper *(Parnu Postimees)* was founded in 1857.

GEORGIANS

The Georgians are descended from an early intermingling of old Caucasian and Mediterranean peoples with others from Asia Minor. In the USSR they number 3.8 million (1985), the majority (3,433,000) living in the Georgian SSR, others in the Azerbaijanian SSR and North Ossetian ASSR. About 150,000 live in Turkey and Iran. Their language belongs to the Kartvelian branch of the Ibero-Caucasian family. Its alphabet, based on the phonetic principle, dates from the 5th c. The majority are members of the independent Georgian Orthodox Church, with a Sunnite Moslem minority.

The Georgian (Gruzinskaya) SSR. Area: 26,911 sq. mi. Capital: Tbilisi (Tiflis). Population (1982): 5.1 million (65% Georgians, the others mostly Armenians, Russians, Ossetians, Azeri). The republic includes the Abkhaz ASSR (pop. 513,000: 83,000 Abkhazians, also Georgians, Russians, Armenians), the Adzhar ASSR (pop. 367,000: 284,000 Georgians, also Russians, Armenians), and the South Ossetian AO (pop. 98,000). Georgia, occupying the west and north-west areas of Transcaucasia, is predominantly mountainous, with the Greater Caucasus range (highest peak, Shkhara, 17,063 ft) in the north and the Lesser Caucasus (highest peak, Bol Abul, 10,830 ft) in the south. Between lie the Kolkhida lowlands (ancient Colchis, land of the Golden Fleece) bordering on the Black Sea, and the higher valleys drained by the Kura, the biggest river, which flows east towards the Caspian Sea. The climate ranges from continental in the north to subtropical in the south, hence the great variety of vegetation and crops. The western part has the highest rainfall in the USSR (over 100 in. annually), while the Kura valley has less than 20 in. The Black Sea area is famous for its tea, citrus and other fruits, vines and tobacco. Livestock raising (cattle, sheep, goats) is important in the highlands. Natural resources include manganese (one of the world's largest deposits), timber, barite, coal and oil. There are numerous mineral springs and abundant sources of hydro-electric power. Metallurgy, engineering, chemicals, timber and food processing are the leading industrial branches. Batumi (an oil terminal), Poti and Sukhumi are the chief Black Sea ports. Tourism is developed on the coast and on Lake Ritsa.

The region formed part of the gold-rich empire of the Colchians in the 6th c. BC, and from the 4th c. BC the kingdom of Iberia, most of which came under Roman sway in the 1st c. BC. Georgia was Christianised c. 330. From the early 6th to the 10th c. it was ruled by the Persian Sassanids, Byzantium and the Arab caliphs, with local vassal kings. In the 11th to 13th c. the Georgian kingdom grew powerful under such rulers as Bagrat III, David the Builder, and Queen Tamara, a golden age ended by the Mongol-Tatar invasions. Turkey and Persia struggled for control of the territory from the 16th to 18th c. The Georgians sought Russian protection, and in 1783 King Irakli (Hercules) II accepted Russian suzerainty under a treaty with Catherine the Great. Part of the territory was annexed by Russia in 1801, and the rest successively up to 1864. In the Russo-Turkish War (1877–78), the Ottoman-ruled areas on the Black Sea were seized. In 1917 a Soviet government was established, and from 1918–21 a counter-revolutionary regime. From 1922 Georgia formed part of the Transcaucasian SFSR, which was broken up into separate republics in 1936.

Though one of the smallest Soviet constituent republics, from the cultural and artistic aspect Georgia is among the richest and most fascinating. After their early conversion to Christianity, the Georgians raised many remarkable churches and monasteries in a style similar to that of neighbouring Armenia, influenced by Hellenistic and Byzantine works, but with many original features (conical domes on tall drums, a variety of complex ground-plans). From the 10th c. on, distinctive Georgian and Armenian styles developed. Among the outstanding Georgian monuments are the monastery church at Djvari (early 7th c.) and the 10th-c. cathedral of

Cathedrals of the Kremlin, Moscow. Engraving.

218

Mtzhet (Mschet), the ancient capital of Georgia. The churches were decorated with sculpture, mosaics and wall-paintings of a high standard. Mediaeval Georgia was also noted for its works of art in metal and enamel, and for its woodcarving. A highly artistic and imaginative people, the Georgians are famous for their folk music and also their athletic skills.

Written literature dates from the 5th c., when parts of the Bible and other religious works were translated. There is an early account of the conversion of Georgia by St Nino, who is credited with inventing the Georgian alphabet. The prosperity of the Georgian kingdom in the 11th–12th c. was accompanied by the flowering of literature. Georgia's greatest poet, Shota Rustaveli (12th c.) wrote his epic *Knight in a Panther's Skin,* dealing with the themes of friendship, love and chivalry. After the Mongol, Persian and Turkish invasions, literature began to revive in the 18th c. Russian annexation had a considerable impact on Georgian culture. The Romantic poet A. Tchavtchavadze (1786–1846) established contact with European literary trends, which then replaced Persian influence. The 'Georgian Byron' N. Baratashvili (1817–1845) wrote the poem *The Destiny of Georgia,* and G. Eristavi laid the foundations of the modern Georgian theatre.

GERMANS

The people of German origin living in the USSR can be divided into several subethnic groups whose ancestors came to settle there in various periods or found themselves within the Russian or Soviet state as a result of frontier changes. They number about 2 million, the majority living in Kazakhstan (900,00), the Russian SFSR (790,000), Kirghizia (100,000), the Altai region and western Siberia. Smaller groups are to be found in the Uzbek, Tadzhik, Ukrainian and Baltic SSRs. The ethnic Germans whose ancestors were invited to settle along the Volga by Catherine II in 1760 were mostly deported to Siberia for anti-Soviet activities in World War II, and the German Volga ASSR (1924–1941) was abolished. The majority live in towns, except in Kazakhstan and Kirghizia, where they are mainly rural. Over 90% are fluent in Russian.

The Germans in the USSR have not retained their national costumes, but their homes often have traditional types of rugs and eiderdowns, and their diet includes typical sausages, dumplings and cakes. Their songs combine German lyrics with Russian or Ukrainian melodies.

JEWS

Soviet Jews, numbering some 1.8 million, are to be found in all parts of the USSR, mostly living in the larger towns, and over half in the western regions (Ukraine, Belorussia, Moldavia, Latvia, Lithuania). The Jewish AO (pop. 200,000; main city: Birobidzhan) in the Khabarovsk district, in the far east of the Russian SFSR, was designated as a homeland for Soviet Jews in 1934, but attracted very few settlers. Over 90% of Soviet Jews are Ashkenazim.

In the 8th c. Judaism was adopted by the emperor (kaghan) and ruling class of the Khazars, a long-vanished people whose empire at that time stretched from the Black Sea to the Urals and middle Volga. From the 10th to 13th c. there were Slavic-speaking Jews in the state of Kievan Rus. These were subsequently assimilated by the Yiddish-speaking Ashkenazim who moved east from Germany in the 16th to 17th c. to escape persecution and the horrors of the Thirty Years' War. Large numbers of Jews were incorporated in the Russian Empire by the division of Poland in the late 18th c. and were confined by law to the western provinces (Pale of Settlement, 1791). Restrictions and persecution eased during the reign of Alexander II, but after his assassination in 1881, Jews were subjected to state-organised pogroms and used as scapegoats to alleviate popular discontent for the rest of the imperial period. This resulted in large-scale emigration, especially to the USA. The Soviet Government abolished all restrictions on Jews and condemned anti-Semitism. In the 1920s and early 30s assimilation intensified, with many Jews adopting Russian in place of Yiddish. In the interwar years, Jews were prominent in political life (Trotski, Zinoviev).

Today more than half of Soviet Jews are employed in educational, cultural, scientific and business activities. The majority are non-practising. Following the recent easing of restrictions on emigration to Israel, a considerable number have left the USSR. Elements of Yiddish culture (theatres, musical groups, literature) have been preserved in the western parts of the country.

KAZAKHS

The Kazakhs, a Turkic-Mongol people, number 7,470,000 (1985) in the USSR, of whom 5,289,000 live in the Kazakh SSR, the others in the Uzbek, Turkmen, Kirghiz and Tadzhik SSRs and in some *oblasts* of the Russian SFSR. In China there are about one million, and in Mongolia, 100,000. Their language belongs to the north-west (Kipchak) group of the Turkic family. They are predominantly Sunnite Moslems.

The Kazakh SSR. Area: 1,050,192 sq. mi. Capital: Alma-Ata. Population (1982): 15,253,000 (30% Kazakhs, Russians, Ukrainians, Germans, Tatars, Uzbeks). The largest Soviet republic after the Russian SFSR, Kazakhstan is mostly semi-arid steppe and desert stretching from the Caspian depression in the west to the mountains of Central Asia in the east (Altai, Dzhungarski Alatau, Tien Shan) with peaks of over 14,000 ft. Between lie lower ranges, the vast Bet-Pak-Dala plateau, deserts, inland seas and great lakes: the north-east part of the Caspian, Aral and Balkash. The chief rivers are the Irtysh, Ural and Syr-Darya (Oxus). The climate is continental and dry. Livestock breeding (cattle, sheep, goats) and grain growing (with irrigation) are the main branches of farming. The republic is rich in mineral resources (copper, lead, zinc, chrome, etc.) and has significant quantities of coal, oil and hydro-electric power. Metallurgy, chemicals and engineering are the main industries.

The Kazakhs formed as a nation in the 15th–16th c. on territory ruled by the Huns, Turks and Mongols. There were three main branches, known as the Great, Middle and Little Hordes, which inhabited the eastern, central and western regions respectively of the present republic. From the 17th to 19th c. these fell in succession under Russian rule as the Empire expanded eastward, though not without resistance, mainly provoked by

settlement of Russian and Ukrainian peasants. The pastoral nomadic Kazakhs began to practise some agriculture in the 19th c., but many remained herders. To distinguish them from the Cossacks *(Kazaki),* the Russians called them Kirgiz, a misnomer that survived down to 1920, when the Soviet Government established the Kirgiz ASR within the Russian SFSR. Its name was changed in 1925, and in 1936 Kazakhstan became a full-fledged republic. In the face of resistance, a policy of settling the nomads was implemented from 1927 on. The Kazakhs also opposed the large-scale settlement of Russians and Ukrainians as part of the New Lands campaign (1954).

The Kazakhs were renowned in the past as tough and intrepid fighters, skilled archers and tireless riders ('The Kazakh is born in the saddle'). Wealth was measured by number of horses, though sheep and goats were the basic livestock. Tribal groups made up of a number of extended families moved with their herds, carrying with them their dome-shaped felt tents *(yurts)*. This life style had virtually disappeared in the Soviet Union by the mid-1930s, but survived into the 1960s in neighbouring China. The first Kazakh newspaper was founded in 1910. In recent decades the development of the republic into an important industrial and grain-growing region of the USSR has created conditions for the advancement of cultural and intellectual activities among the Kazakhs.

KIRGHIZ

The Kirghiz are a Mongoloid people formed out of several South Siberian and Central Asian ethnic groups. In the USSR they number 2.24 million (1985), of whom 1,685,000 live in the Kirghiz SSR, the rest in the Uzbek SSR, Tadzhik SSR (the Pamir Kirghiz) and Kazakh SSR. Others live in China, Afghanistan and Mongolia. Their language belongs to the north-west group of Turkic languages. They are of the Islamic (Sunnite) faith.

The Kirghiz SSR (Kirghizstan). Area: 76,641 sq.mi. Capital: Frunze. Population (1982): 3,724,000 (40% Kirghiz, also Russians, Uzbeks, Ukrainians). It is bordered by three other Soviet republics (Kazakh, Uzbek and Tadzhik), and China (Sinkiang) in the south-east. The whole republic consists of the western part of the great Tien Shan mountain system, and is mostly over 5,000 ft a.s.l. Its loftiest peak, Pobeda (24,406 ft), the second highest in the USSR, lies on the Chinese frontier. The mountains are intersected by two major rivers, the Chu and Naryn. Issyk-Kul is one of the largest (2,394 sq.mi.) and deepest (2,303 ft) mountain lakes in the world. Despite its altitude (5,400 ft), it never freezes (Issyk-Kul = warm lake). The temperate climate of its basin allows the cultivation of the medicinal (opium) poppy and other crops. The natural resources of Kirghizstan include coal, oil, mercury, antimony and other non-ferrous minerals. The most fertile areas are the Kirghiz part of the Ferghana Valley and the area around Frunze. Grain, opium poppy, and industrial crops are grown. Sheep, for wool and meat production, are the main livestock. Besides mining and oil extraction, industry includes textile and leather manufacturing, food processing and metallurgy.

The Kirghiz lived along the upper Yenisei River in the 2nd c. BC, later spreading to the Altai Mts and Lake Baikal area. In the 7th c. they were under the Chinese, and from 758 to 840 under the Uighurs. After a brief period of independence they were vassals of various Chinese and Mongol rulers until they formed a state with the Kazakhs in the late 16th c. Later they were ruled by Dzhungaria, China (1758) and the Khan of Kokand (early 19th c.). Russian expansion eastward brought these parts into the Empire in 1878. Though the Kirghiz had enjoyed no national political rights under the Tsar and much of their fertile land was settled by Russians, they proffered considerable armed resistance to the Soviet Government. Kirghizia was made an AO in 1925, an ASSR in 1926, and a full republic in 1936.

Like the other pastoralists of Central Asia, the Kirhiz had a strong tribal and extended family social structure and were mostly nomadic until the 20th c. But while Kazakh and Turkmen transhumance was north-south, the Kirghiz moved seasonally between higher pastures and secluded valleys. Though now settled, a significant number are still herders, organised in livestock farming collectives.

The Kirghiz have rich folk traditions, notably lyrical poetry, heroic epics and instrumental music, that bear the imprint of their pastoral nomadic past. As among the other Central Asian peoples, bards or folk singers were custodians of the oral literature and much respected members of the community. They memorised thousands of lines of poetry, composed by thesmelves or others, in time creating famous epics such as *Manas* (over 25,000 lines), inspired by the idea of unification of the warring Kirghiz tribes in the face of foreign conquerors. Toktogul Satylganov (1864–1933) and Togolok Moldo (1860–1942) are considered the founders of written Kirghiz literature, which developed only after the Revolution.

LATVIANS (LETTS)

The Latvians or Letts (Latviesi) belong to the Baltic group of the Indo-European family. In the Soviet Union they number 1,445,000 (1985), of whom 1,334,000 (1979) live in the Latvian SSR, the others mostly in the

Russian SFSR and the Lithuanian, Estonian and Belorussian SSRs. There are an estimated 65,000 in the USA, Canada, Sweden and Australia. Their language, Latvian or Lettish, is close to Lithuanian and Old Prussian. The majority are Protestants (Latvian Lutheran Church), with some Roman Catholics, mostly in the Latgale district.

The Latvian SSR. Area: 24,594 sq.mi. Capital: Riga. Population: 2,552,000 (53% Latvians, also Russians, and smaller numbers of Belorussians, Poles and Jews). The central of the three Baltic republics, the country is lowlying, intersected by rivers, with extensive marshes and many small lakes. Its highest point is little more than 1,000 ft. It has 100 mi. of coast on the Gulf of Riga (frozen in winter), into which flows its chief river, the Daugava (Western Dvina), and 100 mi. of Baltic coastline (ice-free most years). The climate is relatively mild for the latitude (Jan. −5 °C, July 17 °C), owing to the maritime influence. Apart from peat, it has few natural resources and relies mainly on neighbouring Soviet republics for power and fuel. Livestock (cattle, pigs, sheep) is more important than arable farming (grain, fodder, flax and other industrial crops). Fishing is significant on the coast. Industry (engineering, textiles, paper, timber working, food processing) is well developed. Tourism is important in the Rigas Jumula area and 'Livonian Switzerland', a scenic hilly area in the east.

In the 2nd millennium BC Baltic peoples settled along the Baltic Sea, in Belorussia and western Russia. In the region of Latvia, the Latgalls, ancestors of the Latvians, subjugated the Ugro-Finnish tribes, Livs, on the coast. When German merchants and missionaries began focussing their attention on the western Baltic coast in the 12th c., they gave the name Livonia to the region that is now Latvia and Estonia. From the early 13th c. the crusading order of Knights of the Sword (soon merged with the Teutonic Knights) overran the country and established a feudal confederation with the Archbishop of Riga and the free city of Riga, which joined the Hanseatic League in 1282. The Latvians were mostly reduced to serfdom. In the 16th and 17th c. the country was divided under Polish and Swedish rule. During the Great Northern War, Peter the Great seized Riga (1710) and gained an opening for Russia onto the Baltic. By the end of the 18th c., all of Latvia had been annexed by Russia. Under Tsar Alexander I, Latvian serfs were emancipated (1817–19), over forty years before the Russian serfs, though unable to purchase the land they worked from their landlords, mostly Germans. At the end of 1917 a Soviet Government was formed in part of Latvia. In the civil war that followed the Government of Karlis Ulmanis eventually triumphed, with the help of Polish and White Guard forces, and concluded a peace treaty with the USSR (1920). The Latvian republic proclaimed in 1922 proved politically unstable, and in 1934 Ulmanis established a dictatorship. Following the German-Soviet accord of 1939, Soviet troops occupied the country in June 1940, and the Latvian SSR was incorporated in the USSR, an act never recognised by the USA and other western nations. From 1941 to 1944 the republic was under German occupation. In the 1940s, over 200,000 Latvians were deported to Russia and 65,000 fled to Germany and Sweden.

Traditionally farmers, herders and, on the coast, fishermen, the Latvians lived in small villages, building their dwellings mostly of wood. Weaving, blacksmithing, pottery and woodworking were the chief crafts. Folklore motifs and traditions are present today in the products of the applied arts: embroidery, knitting, textiles, ceramics, metal and amber objects, and woodcarvings.

Latvian lyrical folk poetry is very rich and of ancient origin. Close to one million songs *(dainas)* and variants have been recorded. The earliest written literature is 16th-c. religious works connected with the Reformation. The Bible was translated in the late 17th c. In the period of 'national awakening' in the mid-19th c., literature began to flourish, often inspired by folk motifs and peasant life: the poet and playwright J. Plieksans-Rainis, the playwright R. Blaumanis, the poet Karlis Skalbe. Social problems and the desire for indepedence were also reflected in the work of writers in the late 19th and early 20th c.

LITHUANIANS

The Lithuanians belong to the Baltic group of the Indo-European family. In the USSR they number 2,985,000 (1985), of whom 2,712,000 live in the Lithuanian SSR. Significant numbers are to be found in Siberia, and also in the USA (est. 330,000), Canada, Poland, South America and Australia. The highly inflected Lithuanian language is close to Latvian. The majority are Roman Catholic.

The Lithuanian SSR. Area: 25,174 sq. mi. Capital: Vilnius. Population (1982): 3,474,000 (85% Lithuanians, also Russians, Poles). The largest of the three Baltic republics, Lithuania (Lietuva, Russian: Litva) is low-lying, with marshy areas, many small glacial lakes, and moraines forming low hills, nowhere exceeding 1,000 ft. Its 50-mi. Baltic coastline has many dunes. The principal river, the Niemen, flows into the large Kurland lagoon, almost cut off from the Baltic by sand-bars. Klaipeda is the main port. Apart from peat, it has virtually no industrial or power resources, and relies on the Russian SFSR for its energy needs. The climate is similar to Latvia's. The main crops are grain, fodder, potatoes, and flax, the basis of the textile industry. Livestock farming (especially dairying) is important. Vilnius is the centre of the engineering industry.

To resist the German orders of knights, in the 13th c. the Lithuanian tribes united under Mindaugas, who was baptised (1251) and crowned by the Pope (1253). The people, however, and subsequent rulers, remained faithful to their traditional gods. Gedimas (ruled 1315–41) founded an extensive empire that included much of Kievan Rus. His grandson Jogaila (Jagiello) was baptised and married the young Queen Jadwiga of Poland (1386), uniting the Polish and Lithuanian realms in a personal union. Full political union was established at Lubin in 1569. The division of Poland in 1795 brought most of ethnic Lithuania into the Russian Empire, which acquired the remaining province of Suvalkai at the Congress of Vienna in 1815, when Tsar Alexander I assumed the title grand prince of Lithuania. In 1918 an independent state was proclaimed while the country was still under German occupation. A government headed by A. Voldemaras was formed, supplanted in 1919, after the entry of the Red Army, by a short-lived Communist Government. The republic became a member of the League of Nations in 1921. After a right-wing coup in 1926, Voldemaras was prime minister and A. Smetona president. In 1940 Lithuania was occupied by the Red Army and incorporated in the USSR. After the German occupation (1941–44), it again became part of the Soviet Union. Large numbers of Lithuanians were deported to Siberia and northern Russia, while Russians were settled especially in the Vilnius and Klapeida areas.

The Lithuanians are predominantly agriculturalists, also engaging in fishing and bee-keeping. Their colourful national costumes are made of wool and linen, elaborately embroidered and ornamented. Oral literature, particularly lyrics, and handcrafts have a rich tradition.

157. A cave chapel of Geghard Monastery, Armenia, one of many built into the cliffs near the monastery in the thirteenth century.

158. War memorial in the Fiagdon Valley, Northern Caucasus. The monument was raised near the place where German forces were thrown back in 1942, following their rapid advance across Russia in the first year of the Great Patriotic War, when they reached as far as the Caucasus.

59. *Towers of the dead in the Fiagdon Valley in North Ossetia. The fortified villages along this valley dating back to the days of the Mongol invasions have towers for all purposes: defence, dwelling and burial. The towers of the dead have no opening except a narrow hole through which a family's corpses were pushed until there was room for no more.*

60. *Symbols of purification at the Monastery of the Holy Lance, Geghard, Armenia. A place of Christian worship since the fourth century, the monastery, some 20 miles from Erivan, is a site of particular holiness for devout Armenians. After worshipping in the church, they leave behind ribbons and cloths, symbols of sin and the powers of evil, tied to surrounding bushes and trees.*

61. *Cathedral of the Nativity of the Virgin, Suzdal. The central building of Suzdal's Kremlin, this magnificent white stone edifice with five star-spangled onion domes was raised in the early thirteenth century. Its renowned Golden Doors are from the same period. Beside it stand a seventeenth-century belfry and the rambling three-storied Bishop's Palace. (pp. 230–231)*

162. *From earliest times wood was the chief building material in most parts of Russia, a land of vast forests where timber was cheap, abundant and ready to hand. Master carpenters raised huge wooden churches, often without the use of nails or any tools other than axes. The wooden verandah is still a feature of many houses built of more durable material, as in this Georgian house.*

163. A Russian village house. Throughout Russia, Belorussia and the Ukraine wood is still widely used for house-building. Between the double walls of planks, wood-shavings or earth provide effective insulation against the bitter cold of winter and summer heat. Houses are often painted bright colours, while the decorative carving framing windows and doors is picked out in white.

164. *Mosque in the Ark, the ancient citadel of the city of Bokhara, with a wooden arcade supported by columns with stalactite capitals.*

165. *Façade of a house in Tbilisi, Georgia, mind-nineteenth century, with typical decorative wooden verandahs.*

166. *Wooden houses perched precariously above the River Kura in Tbilisi.*

167, 168. *Traditional types of wooden dwellings, one Russian (above), the other Georgian.*

169–173. *Examples of the widespread use of wood for a variety of buildings: porch of a Lamaist Buddhist temple in the Buryat Autonomous Republic; school in the Georgian mountain village of Nikortsminda; verandahs of town houses in Tbilisi, Georgia; columned porch of a mosque in Bokhara; rural dwelling in Siberia.*

174. In the old, oriental quarter of Tbilisi, many dwellings with verandahs were built onto or inside the ancient city walls.

175. Wayside gravestone in Ossetia bearing a carved figure of the deceased. The Ossetians are mostly Orthodox Christians with a Moslem minority.

The 'national awakening' came late as Polish or Russian was long used as the official language. Written literature appeared in the 16th c., but was mostly of a religious or didactic character until the latter 19th c., when writers such as V. Kudirka and the poet Maironis appeared. The outstanding figure in the early 20th c. is the novelist and playwright V. Krévé-Mickievičius.

MOLDAVIANS

The Moldavians (Moldovans), like the Rumanians, are of mixed origin, but certainly descended in part from Roman veterans settled in the province of Dacia who intermarried with the local peoples. In the USSR they number 3,165,000 (1985). Moldavian belongs to the eastern group of the Romance branch of Indo-European languages, and is in some respects closer than Italian to the Latin language. The majority are Orthodox Christians.

The Moldavian SSR. Area: 13,000 sq. mi. Capital: Kishinev. Population (1982): 4 milion (63% Moldavians, also Ukrainians, Russians, Jews, Gypsies). The mixed population also includes 3% of Gaguazy, an ethnic group of obscure origin who speak a Turkic language, and some Bulgars, descendents of 18th-c. refugees who fled the Turks. Moldavia (Moldova), the second smallest SSR and most densely populated, lies mostly between the rivers Dniester and Prut, the latter forming the border with Rumania. These and their tributaries intersect the Bessarabian Highlands, which nowhere exceed 1,500 ft. The climate is moderate continental and the soil fertile, providing excellent conditions for varied agriculture (grain, vines, fruit, tobacco, industrial crops), also silkworm culture and bee-keeping. Moldavia is noted in the USSR for its wines. Food processing and distilling are also important. Other industry (engineering) is centred on Kishinev and Beltsy.

The ancient inhabitants, Dacians and Thracian Getae, were Romanised between the 1st and 3rd c. AD. From the 9th to 14th c. the region was successively under the rule of Kievan Rus, the princes of Galicia, and the Tatars. In 1359 the Moldavians under Voivode Bogdan established their own principality, at first a vassal of Hungary, but later independent. Prince Stephen the Great (ruled 1457–1501) managed to hold back the Turks, but from 1511 down to 1859 Moldavia recognised Ottoman rule. In the late 18th and early 19th c., parts were taken by Austria and by Russia, which acquired all Bessarabia up to the Prut by the Treaty of Bucharest (1812). In 1856 it returned the southern part to the principality of Moldavia, which in 1859 entered into a personal union with the principality of Wallachia under Prince Alexander Cuza. From this emerged the state of Rumania (a kingdom from 1881). After the Revolution, Moldavian territory in the USSR (east of the Dniester) was proclaimed an ASSR within the Ukrainian SSR (1924). When Rumania ceded Bessarabia to the USSR in 1940, its larger, central part and the ASSR were united to form the Moldavian SSR. It was occupied by German and Rumanian forces from 1941 till spring 1944, when it was retaken by the Red Army.

In consequence of the eventful history of this part of Europe, the inhabitants of Moldavia are an extraordinary mixture of peoples. Though the Moldavian language is basically Romance, it shows strong Slavic as well as Latin influence. This intermingling is also reflected in customs and physical appearance.

176. The ruins of Pendjikent, Tadzhikstan, with the foothills of the Pamirs in the distance. This Sogdian settlement was founded in the fifth century and abandoned already in the eighth, after the Arab invasion of Central Asia. The excavation of the town, covering 50 acres, has thrown considerable light on pre-Moslem communities of this region. (pp. 238–239)

177. Mausoleum of the Sultan's Mother, Hazreti Shakh-i-Zindeh, Samarkand. This elegant funerary monument with its two domes, one over the tomb, the other above the memorial chamber, was raised in the early fifteenth century as part of the larger complex known as Hazreti Shakh-i-Zindeh (Shrine of the Living Dead). Over the centuries, this grew into a whole street of domed tombs, built on a hillside on both sides of a narrow passageway.

241

MORDVINS

The Mordvins belong to the Ugro-Finnish ethno-linguistic family. In the USSR they number 1.4 million (1985), of whom 340,000 live in the Mordvinian ASSR, the rest mostly in other parts of the Russian SFSR. There are two distinct groups, the Erzya (north and west) and Moksha (south and east), whose dialects differ so greatly that they may be considered two separate languages. They are Orthodox Christians.

The Mordvinian ASSR. Area: 10,200 sq.mi. Capital: Saransk. Population (1982): 974,000 (35% Mordvins, the majority Russians, also Tatars). Part of the Russian SFSR, the autonomous republic lies in the middle Volga basin. The rolling plains and uplands (up to 1,000 ft) are drained by the Moksha and Sura, the principal rivers, and their tributaries. The climate is continental. Agriculture (grain, especially rye, hemp and other industrial crops) forms the basis of the economy. Livestock farming and bee-keeping are also significant. Timber, peat and chalk (for cement) are the chief natural resources. Engineering, timber working, food processing and the manufacture of building materials are the main industries.

A Mordvin tribal alliance of Erzya and Moksha recognised the rule of the Volga Bulgars in the 10th c. In the 13th c. they came under Tatar-Mongol rulers, and from the mid-16th under the Russians, after the destruction of the Kazan khanate by Ivan the Terrible. They were granted some autonomy within the Russian SFSR in 1928, and in 1934 the ASSR was established. Mordvins are outnumbered three to one by Russians.

The Mordvins tend to be tall, dark-haired and blue-eyed, though the Moksha are generally somewhat darker and have some Mongoloid traits. They have preserved their elaborate national costume, worn on special occasions, and their traditional handcrafts, notably embroidery and wood-carving. They have a large body of ritual folk poetry and legends which reflect the old Mordvinian religion of nature worship. Some ancient customs such as bride kidnapping and animal sacrifice survived until very recently. Written literature has developed since the Revolution.

POLES

The ethnic Poles in the USSR, numbering about 1.2 million, mostly live in the Belorussian, Ukrainian, Lithuanian and Latvian SSRs and the Russian SFSR. On the basis of the Potsdam Agreement (1945), Poland's western frontier was shifted to the Oder-Niesse line (a gain of 40,000 sq. mi.) and its eastern frontier was moved west to the Pripet (a loss of 70,000 sq. mi.), thus increasing the Polish population in the USSR, though many Poles were repatriated at that time.

Poles in the USSR have retained some of their rich national culture, noted for its music, oral literary traditions, and crafts (embroidery, knitting, weaving, painting on glass, carving), as they have done to a varying extent in other countries where they are settled: the USA (3.8 million), France (300,000), Canada (255,000) Great Britain (130,000), Brazil and Argentina (120,000 each), Germany (50,000) and elsewhere. They are predominantly Roman Catholics, with some Protestants.

RUSSIANS

The Russians, the largest of the Slav nations, belong to the Eastern Slavic branch. In the USSR they number 143.5 million (1985), of whom 113.5 million live in the Russian SFSR. They also make up a sizeable proportion of the population in other republics (Kazakh 40%, Latvian 33%, Estonian 28%, Kirghiz 26%, Ukrainian 20%, etc.). There are an estimated 1.3 million living abroad, mostly in the USA (1 million), Canada and some European countries. The Russian language is close to Ukrainian and Belorussian. The majority are Orthodox Christians by tradition.

The Russian SFSR. Area: 6.6 million sq. mi. Capital: Moscow (pop: 8.3 million). Population (1982): 140 million (82% Russians, also Belorussians, Ukrainians, Karelians, Tatars, etc.). The SFSR includes 16 ASSRs:

Church attached to the Great Palace at Pushkin, designed by Bartolomeo Rastrelli. Engraving.

Bashkir, Buryat, Chechen-Ingush, Chuvash, Daghestan, Kabardino-Balkar, Kalmyk, Karelian, Komi, Mari, Mordvinian, North Ossetian, Tatar, Tuva, Udmurt, Yakut; 5 autonomous provinces (AOs), 10 national districts (NOs), 6 regions and 49 districts. Covering about three-quarters of the total area of the USSR, it stretches from Finland in the west to the Bering Sea and Sea of Okhotsk in the east. The Ural Mts, separating the North European plain from the West Siberian plain, mark the division between the European and Asian parts of the USSR. Beyond lies the Central Siberian plateau, bordered to the south and east by ranges of high mountains: the Altai (14,800 ft), Sayan, Stanovoy, Verkhoyansk and Kamchat (15,900 ft). The climate ranges from moderate to extreme continental, with a monsoon region in the Far East. The largest of the many great rivers are the North Dvina, Ob, Yenisei and Lena, flowing into the northern seas, the Amur (into the Pacific) and the Volga (into the Caspian Sea). Besides inland seas and large lakes (Caspian, Baikal, Onega, Ladoga), there are many extensive artificial lakes for hydro-electric power. Vegetation zones range from the northern tundra through temperate forests and steppes to semi-arid and desert regions in the south. The central part of European Russia is the most densely populated. The Russian SFSR has about two-thirds of Soviet industry and 90% of its coal reserves. There are rich deposits of iron, manganese and non-ferrous metal ores in the Urals and Siberia, and of oil and natural gas in the Volga-Urals region and north Caucasus. The USSR has the world's largest timber reserves, 80% of which are in Siberia. The SFSR provides about half the country's wheat, sunflower, potatoes, vegetables and meat.

The Russian Soviet Federated Socialist Republic was the name first adopted for the whole Soviet state in 1918. This was changed to the USSR in 1922, and the Russian SFSR thenceforth designated Russia proper, the largest republic of the Union (at that time also comprising the Ukrainian, Belorussian and Transcaucasian SSRs). Its original area of some 8 million sq. mi. was subsequently reduced by the creation of separate Uzbek, Turkmen, Tadzhik, Kazakh and Kirghiz SSRs. Its earlier history is essentially that of the country as a whole, recounted in the text.

From the original Slav homeland between the Vistula and Dnieper rivers, the Russians gradually spread out over a vast territory and intermingled with various non-Slav peoples. Though their culture reveals Germanic, Scandinavian, Byzantine, oriental and other influences, the old Slav-Russian essence has been preserved. National traditions include building in wood and various crafts (woodcarving, weaving, pottery) that display a specific Russian style. They have a distinctive type of folk poetry *(biline)*, folk music (polyphonic singing) and musical instruments *(balalaika, bandura)*. The national costume throughout ethnic Russian territory consists of a linen tunic or long shirt, side-buttoned and drawn in by a belt, leather boots and in winter a fur hat with ear-flaps.

The Russians rank among the foremost nations in their contribution to the world's arts and sciences. Modern literature begins with Pushkin (1799–1837), the greatest Russian poet, and continues with the 19th-c. 'classics': Gogol, Goncharov, Turgenev, Dostoyevski, L. Tolstoi, Chekhov, Gorki and others. Outstanding poets in the late 19th and early 20th c. include Lermontov, Blok, Mayakovski, Esenin, Mandelstam and Akhmatova. The finest achievements of Russian architecture are the many churches raised in the 11th and 12th c. in the old Russian cultural centres (Kiev, Novgorod, Suzdal), where the Byzantine style was adapted to suit national tastes and needs. This was also a great age of ikon and fresco painting. After the period of Tatar conquest, art and architecture revived in the mid-14th c. Rublov, the most famous ikon painter, worked in the first half of the 15th c. A new epoch in Russian art began in the latter 15th c.

when Moscow became the political and artistic centre. Italian artists came to Muscovy, Byzantine traditions weakened, and national and oriental influences increased. The Moscow Kremlin and its many churches mostly date from this period. The reign of Peter the Great ushered in the St Petersburgian period of art and architecture, when national and Byzantine traditions were abandoned in favour of West European styles. In the mid-19th c., composers such as Rimski-Korsakov, Mussorgski, Borodin and Glinka created a Russian style in orchestral and operatic music, drawing on the folk music. Tchaikovski, the greatest Russian composer of the 19th c., achieved a synthesis of European form and Russian feeling. Prokofiev and Shostakovich are the leading 20th-c. composers. In the early 20th c., Russian painters were in the forefront of modern trends (Kandinsky, Malevich, Chagall), but their work was soon condemned as élitist by the Soviet regime, which propagated 'socialist realism' in all branches of the arts and literature. In recent years modern art has been rehabilitated and censorship of writing partially lifted.

TADZHIKS

The Tadzhiks (Tajiks) are descended from the original Iranian (Indo-European) inhabitants of Turkestan and Afghanistan. In the USSR they number 3.5 million (1985), of whom 2.3 million live in the Tadzhik SSR, others in Uzbekistan (600,000), Kirghizia and elsewhere. They form about a third of the population in Afghanistan, and also live in Iran and China. The Tadzhik language, with several dialects, belongs to the Iranian subgroup of the Indo-European family, and is akin to the Persian spoken in Iran and Afghanistan. The majority are of the Islamic (Sunnite) faith.

The Tadzhik SSR. Area: 55,00 sq.mi. Capital: Dushanbe (formerly Stalinabad). Population (1982): 4.1 million (56% Tadzhiks, also Uzbeks, Russians, Tatars). Lying in the south-west of the Asian part of the USSR, bordering on Afghanistan and China, the republic is mostly covered by high mountains with many glaciers and lakes. Mt Communism (24,590 ft) in the northern Pamirs is the highest peak in the Soviet Union. The lower region in the south-east is drained by the Vakhsh, a tributary of the great Amu-Darya (Oxus), which marks most of the frontier with Afghanistan. The north of the republic includes part of the Ferghana Valley, drained by the Syr-Darya (Jaxartes). The climate varies with altitude: hot in the lowlands and perpetually below freezing above 10,000 ft. The chief natural resources are lead and zinc ore, oil, gas, coal and gold. The republic is a leading producer of hydro-electric power in the USSR. The rivers are also used for irrigating half the arable land. Cotton is the main crop, but wheat, barley, rice, fruit and industrial cultures are raised extensively. Livestock include cattle, karacul sheep, angora goats and yaks. Cotton, silk and leather manufacturing and food processing are the principal industries.

Since very ancient times the Persian-speaking Tadzhiks have led a settled existence, living in villages and practising irrigation. In the first millennium BC their territory formed part of the states of Bactria and Sogdiana. After the Persians (6th–4th c. BC), Alexander of Macedon (4th c. BC), and the Turks (from the 6th c.), the area was ruled by Arabs, who gave the Tadzhiks their present name. In the 9th and 10th c. it was under the Tadzhik Samanid dynasty, and in the 13th and 14th formed part of the Mongol Empire of Jenghiz Khan and Timur. From the 16th c. it belonged to the Bokhara emirate, and from 1868 to the Russian Empire. After the

Revolution, fighting between the Soviet army and counter-revolutionary forces continued here until 1923. The Tadzhik ASSR was founded within the Uzbek SSR in 1924, and the Tadzhik SSR in 1929.

The Tadzhiks have traditionally engaged in both arable and livestock farming. Crafts developed in the lowlands, notably the weaving of silk and woollen textiles, and making of jewelry and pottery. The typical settlement is compact, with narrow winding streets flanked by mud and stone dwellings. About a third of the population live in cities and urbanised settlements. Education has made significant progress since the war. Tadzhik State University was founded in 1948.

TATARS

The Tatars (Tartars) are a Turkic people. In the USSR they number 6.6 million (1985), of whom 1.64 million (the Kazan Tatars) live in the Tatar ASSR within the Russian SFSR. Large groups also live in other parts of the Volga region, in the Urals and western Siberia. Most are Sunni Moslems, except for a minority of the Kazan Tatars who adopted the Orthodox Christian faith in the 16th–18th c. Tatar belongs to the western (Kipchak) group of Turkic languages.

The Tatar ASSR. Area: 26,255 sq.mi. Capital: Kazan. Population (1982): 3.5 million (47% Tatars, also Russians, Chuvash, etc.). The country is mostly rolling plain (300–600 ft a.s.l.) intersected by the middle Volga and lower Kama rivers, with some higher land (1,000 ft) in the south. The climate is continental. Natural resources include large amounts of oil and gas, also timber. One third is covered by black earth. The main crops are grain, industrial cultures and vegetables. Livestock raising (cattle, sheep, pigs, horses) is also important. The main industries are engineering, petroleum refining, textiles, footwear, building materials and timber working.

From the 7th c., modern Tataria was part of the extensive khanate of the Volga Bulgars (a Tatar people), overrun in the 13th c. by the Mongols under Batu Khan (grandson of Jenghiz Khan), who founded the Golden Horde. In c. 1430 the Kazan khanate was established and flourished for a century until destroyed by Ivan the Terrible in 1552. The policy of Russification, including conversion to Orthodoxy, conducted by Peter the Great and his successors in the 18th c, led the Tatars to join the Pugachov rebellion, in which they played a prominent role. After the Revolution and defeat of the White Russian forces, who made Kazan a stronghold, the Tatar ASSR was founded in 1920.

From the anthropological viewpoint, the Tatars differ widely: those of the middle Volga and Ural regions are predominantly of European type, while many of the Astrakhan and Siberian Tatars bear a closer resemblance to the Mongol peoples. The name Tatar was applied very loosely by the Russians to most of the Turkic peoples within the Empire, and even to all Moslems. The Crimean Tatars (c. 400,000) live mostly in the Uzbek SSR (Ferghana and Tashkent areas), in parts of the Krasnodar and Stavropol districts, and also in the Crimean and Kherson *oblasts*. After the formation of the Crimean ASSR (1921), the process of Tatar ethnic consolidation intensified. In 1944 the Crimean Tatar ASSR was abolished and the Tatar population deported to Central Asia as punishment for collaboration with the German occupation forces. Many were prevented from returning, and their civil rights were not restored until 1967.

Tatar folk literature is rich and varied: tales, poems, riddles, proverbs, and the very popular *baiti*, works of an epic or lyrical epic character dealing with historical events. The folk music is similar to that of other Turkic peoples, especially the Bashkirs. Professional cultural activities (literature, music, theatre) have developed since the Revolution. Because of their long contact, the Tatars are the most Russianised of the Turkic peoples of the USSR.

TURKMEN

The Turkmen (Turkomans) belong to the south-west or Oghuz branch of the Turkic peoples. In the USSR they number 2.4 million (1985), of whom 1.9 million live in the Turkmen SSR, others in the Uzbek and Tadzhik SSRs and the Astrakhan region. Their language, one of the western Turkic group, is closer to Turkish and Azerbaijanian than to the languages of the other Turkic-speaking peoples of Central Asia. They are of the Islamic (Sunnite) faith.

The Turkmen SSR. Area: 188,400 sq.mi. Capital: Ashkhabad. Population (1982): 2.97 million (67% Turkmen, also Russians, Uzbeks and others). About half the republic is covered by the Kara Kum (Black Desert). Along the southern border with Afganistan and Iran the Kopet Dagh range rises to over 9,600 ft. Of the rivers, only the Amu-Darya, flowing northward parallel with the Uzbek border, has enough water to cross the Kara Kum. The Caspian Sea, 92 ft below sea level, forms the republic's western border. The large Gulf of Kara-Bogaz-Kul, only 30 ft deep, on the northern part of the Caspian coast, is a rich source of salts, which are industrially exploited. The continental desert climate, with a rainfall of only 4 to 8 in. annually in most places, allows only desert and

Pre-Lenten festivities in Moscow in the late eighteenth century. Engraving.

247

arid steppe vegetation to survive without irrigation, for which large canals have been built across the Kara Kum. Cotton is the principal crop. Silkworm culture is also significant. As the formerly nomadic pastoral population has become settled, there has been a decline in the number of livestock (karacul sheep, goats, cattle, horses, asses and mules, camels). The republic has rich deposits of oil, gas and various salts, also coal, lead, zinc and copper. The chemical, petrochemical and textile industries are of primary importance. Krasnovodsk is the main Caspian port.

The Turkmen, a group of the Seljuk Turks, reached the region from the west in the 11th c., though a kindred people, the Oghuz, probably arrived there much earlier. The territory was under the Mongols in the 13th c., and from the 16th was ruled by the Khiva, Bokhara and Persian states. Their control, however, was mainly confined to the oasis towns, while the pastoral Turkmen pursued undisturbed their semi-nomadic patriarchal way of life which was best suited to this arid terrain. From the mid-19th c. the Russians started penetrating the region and after prolonged campaigns, in which the Turkmen displayed their Seljuk warrior qualities, finally subdued it in the 1880s. After the Revolution, the Red Army fought for control over the area until 1920. The Turkmen SSR was established in 1924, at the same time as other Soviet republics of Turkestan, which was split up in order to prevent the emergence of a strong republic of Turkic peoples within the USSR.

Like the other peoples of Central Asia, the Turkmen have a highly developed oral literature: epic poetry, myths and folk songs, in which Islamic influence is strongly felt. They have preserved traditional crafts, most notably the making of their famous rugs and of beautifully ornamented enamelled metal objects. In the past they moved with their tents and livestock to winter, spring and summer grazing land, living in extended family groups. With the expansion of irrigation, increased fertilisation, and industrial development, they have abandoned their traditional way of life, still followed by Turkmen in neighbouring countries. Over half now live in cities and urban-type settlements. Before World War I, 99% were illiterate. In the 1920s, Arabic script was replaced by Latin, to counteract Turkish political influence. When Turkey adopted the Latin alphabet, the Soviet Government decreed that Turkmen and the other Turkic languages of the USSR should be written in Cyrillic script, as they are today.

UKRAINIANS

The Ukrainians belong to the eastern group of Slav peoples. In the USSR they number 43.5 million (1985), of whom 36.5 million live in the Ukrainian SSR, most of the others in the Russian SFSR and the Kazakh, Moldavian and Belorussian SSRs. There are many Ukrainians living in the USA (500,000), Poland (300,000), Argentina (100,000) and some European countries. The majority are Orthodox, with some Catholics. Their language is close to Russian and Belorussian.

The Ukrainian SSR. Area: 230,000 sq.mi. Capital: Kiev. Population (1982): 50.3 million (77% Ukrainians, also Russians, Poles, Jews). The greater part of the republic comprises a steppe-covered plateau, rising in places to 1,300 ft, and the plains drained by the principal rivers, the Dnieper, Dniester and Southern Bug, all flowing into the Black Sea. In the north lie the marshy lowlands of Polesye and forested regions, in the west

179. *Children enjoying the ice and snow in Novosibirsk. This fast-growing Siberian city now has a population of over one and a half million. Despite the ferocious climate, high building costs, and appalling difficulties of transport and communication, much has been done to attract new settlers. Wages are high, consumer goods are in better supply than in Moscow.*

*180. Zagorsk. The Orthodox faithful
come from all over Russia to drink from
this spring within the walls of the
Troitse-Sergieva Monastery. Its water,
trickling from the arms of a cross, is
believed to heal the sick and give added
vigour to the healthy.*

181. *A tea-house in Bokhara. Tea – the green variety – is the most popular drink of the Moslem Uzbeks, and the tea-house the favourite meeting place of the older men. The Soviet Union is one of the world's major tea growers, but produced only just enough to meet home demand.*

182. *Restaurant-car of the Moscow–Tbilisi express. Despite the growth of internal air transport, railways remain the most important means of travel across the huge expanses. There are half a million miles of wide-gauge track. This extra width, about a third more than the European standard guage, allows greater space and comfort, especially for sleeping, on the long journeys.*

253

183. *Street musicians in Tbilisi. This form of entertainment is very popular in the towns and villages of Georgia, where folk songs and dances are still part of everyday life.*

184. *A flute-player in Ashkhabad, Turkmenistan.*

85, 186. *Weavers in Azerbaijan. Rug and carpet making, the craft passed down from one generation to the next, is an important cottage industry in the Caucasus and Soviet Central Asia. Fine rugs have been woven in the Caucasus since ancient times, notably the famous Dragon carpets once made in the town of Kuba. In Azerbaijan, the influence of the Turkish style is now more pronounced than the old Caucasian traditions in this craft.*

187. The author picnicking with Georgian friends. Famous for their hospitality, the Georgians have a high appreciation of good food and good company. The excellent local wines and brandy certainly contribute to the enjoyment.

188. *A cook at work in a small restaurant in Tashkent. Under the watchful eye of a customer he prepares a local meat speciality. Uzbek cooking is noted for the variety of its ingredients and dishes, with pilaff the most popular.*

89. Members of the Georgian National Dance Company.

190. A Kirghiz village kindergarten. Learning the national songs and dances is considered an important part of aesthetic education. The Soviet Union developed an extensive network of pre-school institutions: crêches for the under-threes and kindergartens for the three to seven age group, attended by some 20 million children.

191. *Evening service in an Orthodox church. The Russians have always been an intensely religious people, and all efforts to replace Orthodoxy by Marxism-Leninism have ultimately proved futile.*

192. *Dushanbe, Tadzhikstan, Gathered before a mosque, the faithful listen to the teachings of a mullah. The past decade has brought an upsurge of Islamic militancy among the 60 million Soviet Moslems, particularly in Azerbaijan and the Central Asian republics.*

193. *A family wedding picture taken in front of the Georgian Patriarch's residence after the ceremony in Sioni Cathedral, Tbilisi.*

194. *Gelati Monastery, Georgia.*
A priest blesses the congregation at
a service marking the church's feast-day.
Important days in the church calendar
are celebrated by special services and
festive events in the churchyard, making
them social as well as religious
occasions.

195. *Another happy couple who wished*
their marriage vows to be sanctified in
church pose with their guests in front of
the holy Nakladeznaya spring in the
Troitse-Sergieva Monastery, Zagorsk.

196. *Tbilisi, Georgian National Dancers perform a stylised version of a folk dance. The company's international reputation owes much to a dedicated and talented couple, Nino and Ilike Sukhisivili, who joined it just after the war and developed it to its present high standard.*

197. The Georgian National Dance Company on stage. Many of the Georgians' national characteristics – elegance, gaiety and dash – emerge in their dancing.

198. *Zagorsk. Newly-weds after the ceremony in one of the churches of the Troitse-Sergieva Monastery.*

199. *A peasant selling pomegranates at Bokhara bazaar. In the fertile regions of their republic, aided by irrigation the Uzbeks grow a large variety of fruit.*

200. *An Uzbek woman. Islamic concepts are deeply ingrained in the Uzbek way of life. Women in towns and villages formerly lived in separate parts of the house, which they could leave only with their husband's permission.*

201. *Pupils of a Moscow school. Their uniform for special occasions dates back to the era of the October Revolution.*

202. *A model poses for the author after a fashion show in Moscow. For a privileged few, Russian haute couture is available; others must make do with dowdy off-the-peg garments.*

203. *Lado Gudiashvili, the eminent Georgian painter.*

267

204–209. *Portraits of Soviet citizens. Different geographical, climatic, economic and historical conditions, combined with migrations and intermingling of peoples, have produced an enormous diversity of types and individuals.*

204. *His Holiness the Most Venerable Bandido Khambo Lama, Chief Lama of all Buddhists in the Soviet Union.*

205. *An Uzbek from Shakrisabz, Tamerlane's birthplace.*

206. *Schoolgirls in Gorki Park, Moscow.*

207. *Students of the Kutaisi Music Academy, Georgia.*

208. *Boys from the Northern Caucasus.*

209. *A Russian-Siberian.*

210, 211. *Herders in Kirghizia, which has some ten million sheep and two million horses, yaks and camels. Apart from the Ferghana Valley and the area around the capital Bishkek (formerly Frunze) the republic has little arable land.* (pp. 269–271)

212. *Portrait of a Buryat lama. The Buryats, members of a north Asian branch of the Mongol race, number around 400,000 half of them living in the Buryat Autonomous Republic within the Russian Federation. The majority are Lamaist Buddhists.*

*213. Kirghiz wrestling on horseback, the
aim being to unseat your opponent. This
sport calls for a combination of strength,
wrestling skill, and excellent
horsemanship.*

214. *Turkmen, members of a nation numbering some two and a half million, most of them living in newly independent Turkmenia.*

215. *A Kirghiz family in front of their yurt. This portable felt tent, home to the nomadic herders of Central Asia down to the early twentieth century, was pitched in seasonal settlements (auls) of one to two hundred tents. The yurt is still used in summer, when the livestock are taken to the high pastures, but the herders now have permanent dwellings in the valleys.*

216. A Turkmen herdsman near the ruins of Merv, the oldest city in the world. It was left deserted in the late eighteenth century when neighbouring Bokharans diverted the nearby Murgab River, turning the once flourishing oasis into arid wilderness.

217. Sheep supply the poorer Kirghiz with most of their needs: wool for their homespun cloth, blankets and rugs, sheepskin for jackets and hats, milk for cheese, yoghurt and other dairy produce so important in the Kirghiz diet.

218. An elderly Tadzhik in traditional dress: a quilted kaftan narrowing slightly at the waist, worn over a similar jacket drawn in by a cummerbund or belt, and wide trousers.

219. While the horse is the prestige animal in Central Asia, asses and mules usually do the 'donkey work', carrying heavy loads and often their owners as well. The sturdy ass, originally from the Arabian peninsula, is highly suited to the arid and rugged terrain of these regions.

220. In the bazaar in Samarkand, for centuries an important trading post and caravan halt on the Silk Road. In addition to farm produce, its markets are always well supplied with all manner of goods. Even more fascinating for the European visitor is the variety of people buying and selling here: Uzbeks, Kazakhs, Tadzhiks, Turkmen and Slavs.

278

the Carpathians (over 6,000 ft), in the south the highlands of the Crimean peninsula (5,000 ft). The republic includes much of the Sea of Azov.

The climate is mostly moderate continental, and Mediterranean on the Black Sea coast. The Ukraine with its large areas of black earth is the 'bread-basket' of the USSR, and ranks second to the Russian SFSR in economic importance. Besides grain, it grows large quantities of industrial crops, vines and fruit. Livestock farming (cattle, pigs) and fishing are also important. Natural resources include coal, iron, oil, gas and timber. Timber working, textiles, engineering and food processing are the main industries. The Crimea is the leading Soviet tourist region. Odessa is the largest Soviet Black Sea port, and Zhdanov the main port on the Sea of Azov.

The territory of the present Ukrainian SSR was inhabited in very ancient times. The Cimmerians who settled there early in the 1st millennium BC were overrun by the Scythians in the 7th c.
From the 4th to 2nd c. BC the Sarmathians dominated the steppes from the Urals to the Danube. Greek colonies were founded on the shores of the Black Sea and Sea of Azov from the 6th c. BC. In the period of great migrations of peoples from the 3rd c. on, the region was on the route taken by the Goths, Huns, Bulgars (5th c.), Avars (6th c.) and Khazars (7th c.). Some historians consider the Ukraine to be the original homeland of the Slavs, who began to establish tribal alliances here from the 4th c. on. In the 8th and 9th c. the settlements of Kiev, Chernigov, Pereslavl and others grew up. The first true state of the East Slavs, Kievan Rus, was founded here in the 9th c. The text provides an account of the further history of the Ukraine, which was under Lithuanian and Polish rule until the mid-17th c., when it was divided between Poland and Russia along the Dnieper. The whole of the Ukraine, except for parts under Austrian rule, was incorporated in the Russian Empire in 1793, when it lost all vestiges of autonomy. An independent Ukrainian SSR was proclaimed in 1918, but Polish, White Guard and Ukrainian national forces battled with the Red Army on this territory until the Peace of Riga (1921), whereby the western Ukraine was assigned to Poland. The following year the Ukrainian SSR entered into a federation with Russia, Belorussia and Transcaucasia, forming the USSR. From 1941, it was under German occupation. A strong partisan guerrilla movement developed, and together with the Red Army liberated the republic in 1944. The Transcarpathian region was ceded to the USSR by Czechoslovakia in 1945. The borders of the Ukrainian SSR were finally demarcated in 1954, when the Crimea was transferred from the Russian SFSR.

A major role in Ukrainian (and Russian) history was played by the Cossacks (from the Turkic word *kazak* meaning 'rebel'), originally peasants who had fled serfdom to settle in the border region *(Ukraina)* between Poland and Russia in the late Middle Ages. Besides Slavs, they included many of Turkic and mixed origin. The Cossacks, their villages organised so that they could muster military forces when necessary, served as Polish frontier guards against the Tatars in the early 16th c., and were later used by the tsars to defend their borders and for the eastern expansion of the Empire. Eminent Cossacks include Yermak Timofeevich, the conqueror of Siberia, Pugachov, leader of the 18th-c. peasant rebellion, and Ivan Mazepa, the Cossack hetman who tried to unite the Ukraine in the time of Peter the Great. Cossack life is described in Gogol's *Taras Bulba* and L. Tolstoi's *The Cossacks*. In the early 20th c., there were 12 Cossack armies in various parts of the Empire.

The Ukrainians, formerly known as Ruthenians *(Rusyny),* have an extremely rich folk literature: legends, heroic poems *(dumy),* ballads and lyrics, as well as a distinctive folk music. The national costume of homespun

221. A young Kirghiz in the saddle. Children in Kirghizia learn to ride as soon as they can walk, and from an early age help to tend the horses, which are of the Mongol breed, noted for its quickness and stamina.

cloth is richly embroidered. The traditional homestead was the thatched log-cabin.

Modern Ukrainian literature in the vernacular began to flourish in the 19th c. with the great poet Taras Shevchenko (1814–1861), M. Sashkevich (in the Polish Ukraine), P. Kulish (translator of the Bible and Shakespeare), M. Vovchok, Ivan Franko and many others. It suffered a period of suppression by the Soviet Government in the 1920s, and several outstanding writers (M. Kulish, M. Zerov) were deported.

UZBEKS

The Uzbeks are a Turkic people, like their neighbours to the west, the Kazakhs, to the east, the Kirghiz, and to the south-west, the Turkmen. In the USSR they number 14.8 million (1985), of whom 10.5 million (1979) live in Uzbekistan, the rest in adjoining Central Asian republics. Over one million live in neighbouring Afghanistan. They are of the Islamic (Sunnite) faith.

The Uzbek SSR. Area: 158,000 sq.mi. Capital: Tashkent. Population (1982): 16.6 million (62% Uzbeks, also Kara-Kalpaks, Russians, Tatars, Kazakhs, Tadzhiks). In the west of the republic lies the Kara-Kalpak ASSR (area 64,000 sq.mi.; capital Nukus: pop. c.550,000), inhabited mostly by Kara-Kalpaks, another Turkic people. From the Aral Sea and Kisil Kum (Red Sands) in the west, the republic extends eastward to the Ferghana Valley, separated by the Chatkal range. The western spurs of the Tien Shan Mts occupy the southern part. The principal rivers are the Syr-Darya (Jaxartes), which flows north-west from the Ferghana Valley into the Aral Sea, and the Amu-Darya (Oxus), which has often changed its course before reaching the southern Aral shore. The climate is continental, with a tremendous range of temperature in some parts. The lowland vegetation is of steppe type, while the mountains are forested. Uzbek is an important cotton-growing region (27% of Soviet production). Vines, rice, fruit and vegetables are grown, primarily in the Ferghana Valley, with the aid of irrigation. Karacul sheep are raised on the steppes. The rich natural resources include oil, gas, non-ferrous minerals, salt and sulphates (Aral Sea). Metallurgy, textiles, chemicals and food processing are the main industrial branches. The ancient cities of Samarkand, Bokhara and Tashkent attract foreign tourists.

Turkestan, of which Uzbekistan forms part, has lain in the path of many conquerors and formed part of various empires since the time of the ancient Persians (6th-4th c. BC) and Alexander of Macedon (4th c. BC). From the 7th c., Arabs, Persians, a Turkic khanate, Seljuks and Mongols ruled it in turn. In the late 15th and early 16th c., it was inhabited by Uzbek tribes, whose name derives from Uzbek (Uzbeg), Khan of the Golden Horde. From their intermingling with the earlier inhabitants of the region, the Uzbek nation was gradually formed. In the 16th c. there were two great Uzbek khanates, Bokhara and Khiva. In the 18th c., a third, the khanate of Kokand, was created. Between 1865 and 1876 all these were absorbed by the Russian Empire, which had been trying to conquer them since the time of Peter the Great. After the Revolution, Communists and Moslem nationalists struggled for control of Turkestan, which was proclaimed an ASSR in 1918. The Uzbek SSR was established in 1924.

The Uzbeks living in the oases traditionally engaged in agriculture, aided by irrigation systems of very ancient origin, crafts and trade. The influence of Islam was very strong, particularly among the settled Uzbek population, and women played a completely subordinate role in society. Marriage was contracted when the bride was 13 or 14, and the groom 15 or 16. To avoid fragmentation of land, marriage between relatives was customary. Social changes following the Revolution led to the breakdown of tribes and extended families.

Uzbek literature has its origins in ancient oral tradition. Many proverbs and sayings recorded by Mahmud Kashgari in the 11th c. are still in use today. Under Arabic influence, mystic religious poetry was written from the 12th c., and didactic prose from the 14th. The finest work of old Uzbek literature is by the poet Alishar Navoi (1441-1501), who exerted a strong influence on its later development. Works of historical importance are *Babur-name* (Babur's Chronicle) by Zahireddin Muhammed Babur (1485–1530), describing Uzbek military campaigns against Afghanistan and India, and *Shaibani-name,* by the poet Muhammed Saih (1455–1506), recounting the conquests of Shaibani-Khan.

The Kremlin, Moscow. Engraving.

Chronology

6th c. BC	First Greek settlements on the Black Sea coast
4th–3rd c. BC	Foundation of the Armenian Empire
2nd–4th c.	Rise of the Georgian kingdom, which adopts Christianity (*c.* 330).
5th c.	Start of migrations of the Slavs
6th c.	First recorded mention of the Russians
7th–10th c.	Khazar Empire rules from the Black Sea to the Urals
9th c.	Foundation of the old Russian state, Kievan Rus, under princes of the Varangian Rurik dynasty
988	Christianity adopted as the Russian state religion
1219–1223	Jenghiz Khan conquers Central Asia and invades Russia, the Ukraine and the Caucasus
1237	Second Mongol-Tatar invasion. Russian cities become vassals of Batu Khan, leader of the Golden Horde
1240	Creation of the Lithuanian grand principality
1325–1340	Rise of Muscovy under Prince Ivan I Kalita
1380	Grand Prince Dmitri Donskoi crushes a Mongol-Tatar army at the Battle of Kulikovo
1462–1505	Ivan III (the Great) rules Muscovy and raises the Kremlin walls and churches
1480	Russia formally freed from vassalage
1535–1584	Reign of Ivan IV (the Terrible), proclaimed Tsar of All the Russias in 1547. Russian Empire expands eastwards with the destruction of the Kazan khanate
1584–1598	Reign of Fyodor I, last of the line of Rurik
1598–1605	Reign of Boris Godunov
1598	Siberia becomes part of the Russian Empire
1613	Michael (Mikhail) Romanov proclaimed tsar.
1654	Unification of Russia and the Ukraine
1682–1725	Reign of Peter I (the Great)
1703	Foundation of St Petersburg, which becomes the new capital (1712)
1709	Peter I defeats the Swedes at Poltava and gains a permanent outlet to the Baltic Sea
1773	Peasant rebellion led by Pugachov
1812	Napoleon's Russian campaign. Battle of Borodino and occupation of Moscow

1812–1814	Liberation of Russia under the leadership of General Kutuzov, counter-offensive, and occupation of Paris
1817–1864	Caucasian wars. Russia occupies north-west Caucasia, Chechen and Daghestan
1825	December Conspiracy, abortive coup by the liberal aristocracy (Dekabrists)
1825–1855	Reign of Nicholas I
1828–29	Russo-Turkish War. Southern frontier consolidated
1853–56	Crimean War. Territorial gains on frontier with Turkey
1858–60	Far Eastern provinces wrested from China
1861	Alexander II decrees the abolition of serfdom
1881	Assassination of Alexander II by People's Will organisation
1905	Russia defeated in war with Japan Widespread rebellion and unrest forces Alexander III to agree to a constitutional assembly *(Duma)*
1914	Germany declares war on Russia
1917	Year of revolution: abdication of Tsar Nicholas II, Provisional Government under Kerenski, victory of the Bolsheviks led by V. I. Lenin
1918	Congress of Soviets formed. Russia withdraws from the First World War
1924	Death of Lenin. J. V. Stalin takes over power
1939	Soviet-German pact signed
1941	Germany attacks the Soviet Union
1942–43	Battle of Stalingrad
1945	Germany defeated, at the cost to the Soviet Union of over 20 million lives
1953	Death of Stalin. N. S. Krushchov eventually emerges as new Soviet leader
1964	Khrushchov ousted. L. I. Brezhnev assumes leadership
1982	Death of Brezhnev, succeeded by Y. V. Andropov, and a year later by K. U. Chernenko
1985	M. S. Gorbachov becomes Party Secretary on Chernenko's death
1991	Dissolution of the USSR, formation of the Commonwealth of Independent States, resignation of M. S. Gorbachov

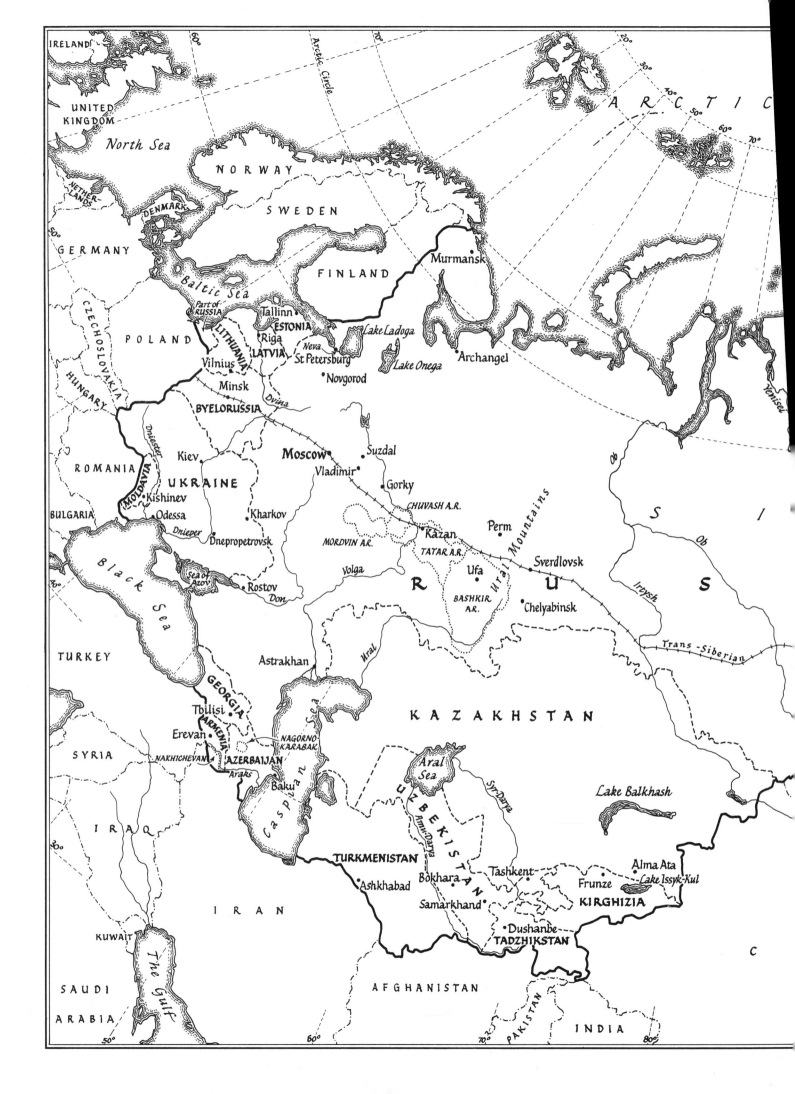

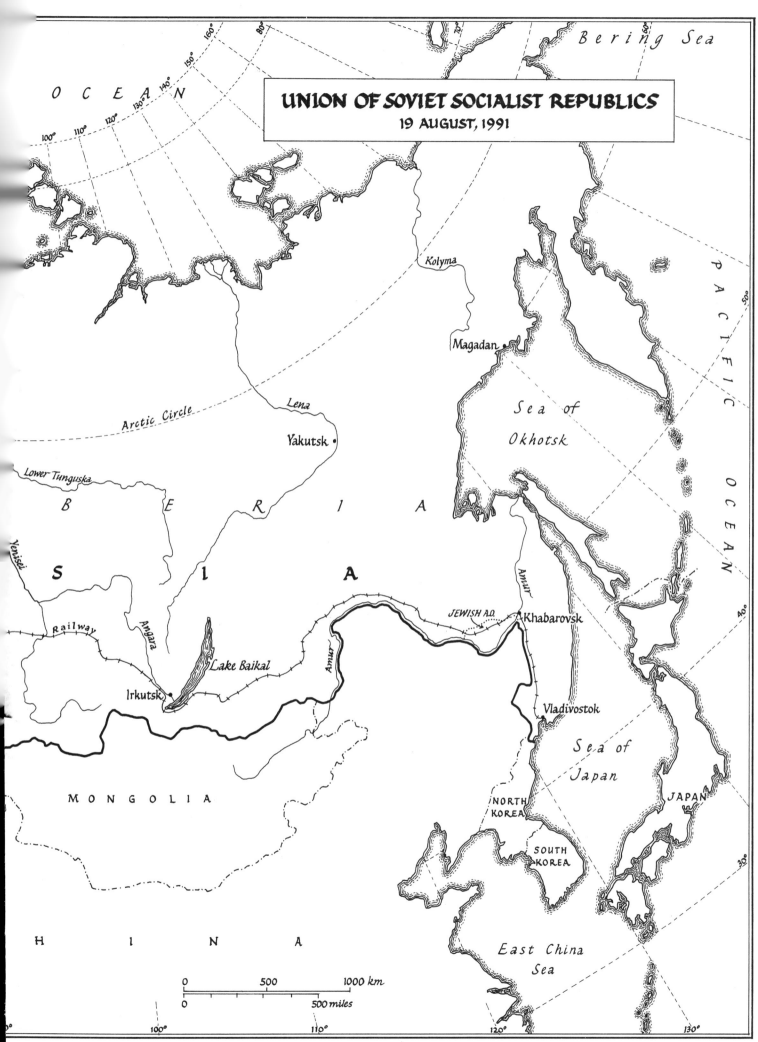

Bering Sea

OCEAN

PACIFIC OCEAN

Kolyma

Magadan

Sea of
Okhotsk

Arctic Circle

Lena

Yakutsk

Lower Tunguska

B   E   R   I   A

Yenisei

S   I   A

Amur

Railway

Angara

Lake Baikal

Amur

JEWISH A.O.

Khabarovsk

Irkutsk

Vladivostok

MONGOLIA

Sea of
Japan

JAPAN

NORTH
KOREA

SOUTH
KOREA

H   I   N   A

East China
Sea

0   500   1000 km

0   500 miles

Index

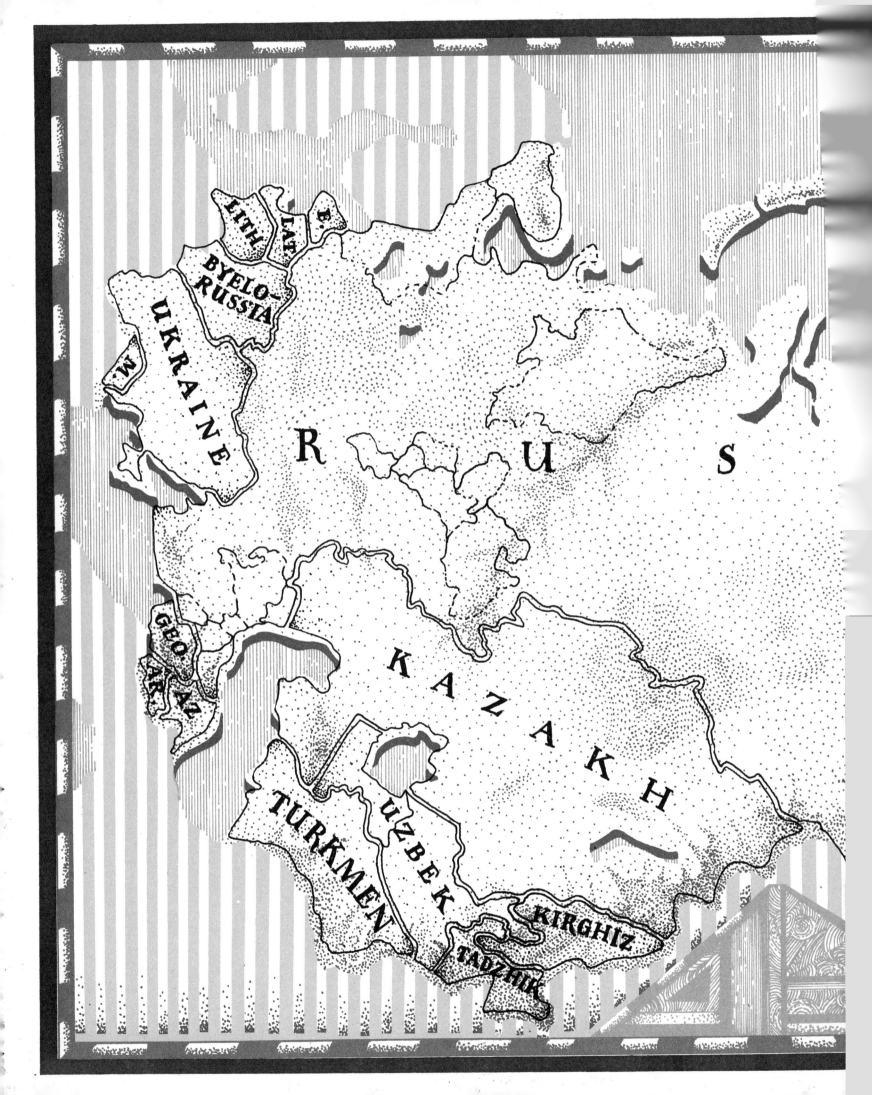